Annie R. Taylor

Pioneering in Tibet

Annie R. Taylor

Pioneering in Tibet

ISBN/EAN: 9783742834805

Manufactured in Europe, USA, Canada, Australia, Japa

Cover: Foto ©Andreas Hilbeck / pixelio.de

Manufactured and distributed by brebook publishing software
(www.brebook.com)

Annie R. Taylor

Pioneering in Tibet

Pioneering in Tibet.

BY

ANNIE R. TAYLOR.

The Origin and Progress of
"THE TIBETAN PIONEER MISSION,"
TOGETHER WITH
My Experiences in Tibet, and
Some Facts about the Country.

LONDON: MORGAN AND SCOTT,
Office of "The Christian,"
12, PATERNOSTER BUILDINGS, E.C.
And may be Ordered of any Bookseller.

A RETROSPECT.

I WAS born in Egremont, Cheshire, and am the second child in a family of five sons and five daughters. My governesses and nurses say that I was a most troublesome child, and very full of mischief. When about seven years of age, the doctor discovered that I had valvular disease of the heart. Two years later I had an attack of acute bronchitis, when my life was despaired of; and this further affected my heart. Then the doctors advised that I should not be troubled with study, as they did not expect me to live to grow up. So for some years I did much as I liked, until in 1869, when at the age of thirteen, I was converted at a small Congregational chapel in Kingston-on-Thames. I had been in the habit of going to church or chapel; but the only part of the sermon to which I listened was that addressed to *sinners*, which I mentally called *my part*.

One Sunday, when kneeling down as others did at the close of the service, a voice seemed to say to me, " If that is *your* part of the sermon, it is *your own choice*, because Christ died for *you*." I there and then 'accepted Him as my Saviour : and on reaching home, I took the Bible to my room and decided to follow whatever God should teach me through His Word. Soon I found that I could no longer take rides on horseback with my father on the Lord's Day ; and this naturally annoyed him.

At the age of sixteen I went to school at Clarence House, Richmond, where I heard an address on Missionary work given by a son of Dr. Moffat. At that time he seemed to think that women were more of a hindrance than a help to Missionary work in Africa. I was longing to be a Mis-sionary ; and felt then, for the only time in my life, sorry that I was a girl. At a meeting held by Lord Radstock, Miss Emsley (soon after the wife of Dr. Barnardo) placed her hand upon my head and asked me, " When are you going to work for Jesus?" I said, " Now ; " and the next day I remember walking through the back streets of Richmond to find some poor person to give ten shillings to ; but finding no one, I came home quite disappointed.

We had been very intimate with the Emsley family, and the life and work of Miss Emsley made a deep impression upon me,

At about eighteen I went to a school in Berlin ; but after a few months my mother was obliged to fetch me home, as I was again taken ill, suffering from my heart. My parents were then staying at Brighton, and there I began to work for Jesus. I found a poor girl who was dying of consumption, and visited her almost every day. Then I heard of another young girl suffering from cancer, and also visited her. When we moved to London, I began to work in a Sunday-school ; and also took a district which had not hitherto been visited. A good part of the day I spent in studying art, being very fond of painting ; and for a time I pursued art studies in Italy. Before going to Germany I gave up theatres, because I could not be happy in any gathering where my Lord was not found. And later on, when in London, I gave up going to dances, having ceased to find any pleasures apart from Jesus. My family were very much annoyed at this; for at that time they had no sympathy with me in my Christian life and work. One evening in 1883, when I returned home from work, my father remonstrated with me, and told me I was selfish. I asked him what he wanted me to do. He answered, "Give up the Mission work, and go into society, like your sisters." This I refused to do; but said, "If you will let me, I will go out to the Mission field, and give my whole life to the work." He then said, "Go!"—little thinking that I really would. I was overjoyed, and at once set about to prepare for this work, going first to the London Hospital for medical training. After that, I went to Queen Charlotte's Hospital, my father having previously promised to pay the fees; but when the time came, he refused to pay the money unless I promised that I would not go anywhere without his permission. He said he was quite willing I should go abroad as a nursing sister in the Army; but not as a Missionary. This I declined to do, as he had previously given me permission to go; he then refused to give me the fees, and stopped my dress allowance. At that time I was twenty-eight; and so, nothing daunted, I sold some of my jewellery; and, living in a small garret, I took my turn in attending to the indoor patients at Queen Charlotte's Lying-in Hospital, and attended numerous cases outside. After passing my examination in midwifery, I returned home. The Lord had met with my mother in a little Italian chapel in Sicily, where she was spending the winter; so I had the joy of having her blessing before leaving for work in China. I had been accepted as a worker by the China Inland Mission. (The friendship of Mr. and Mrs. Hudson Taylor is one of the joys of my life, and their letters of love and sympathy I still continue to receive. This is indeed a cheer amidst the hardships of Pioneer work.)

Some weeks previous to my leaving England, my father had started on a journey to America *en route* for Australia, accompanied by my mother and one of my sisters. He left word that he would pay for anything I bought to take away with me, as he did not want me to lack comforts. He also gave me two letters for different shipping companies which had promised to give me a passage from China to England or Australia, if I should apply for one. He thought I should soon get tired after a few months of Mission work in China, and he no longer continued my allowance. I left for China in October, 1884. A friend, Nellie Barclay, was one of the party; she had been for some time governess to the children of my dearest friend, Mrs. Paterson, the wife of Dr. Sinclair Paterson. Miss Barclay and I were for a time together in China; but I had always realized that Tibet, *not* China, was my goal. How God opened up the way for me to begin work amongst the Tibetans, and then to enter the land, is told in the following pages. I am thankful to add that my dear father, who is a member of the Royal Geographical Society, is now in sympathy with my Pioneer work, and he came out to India to see me. Two of my sisters and a brother-in-law have also paid me a visit in my far-off home in Tibet.

A. R. T.

CONTENTS.

LIST OF ILLUSTRATIONS.

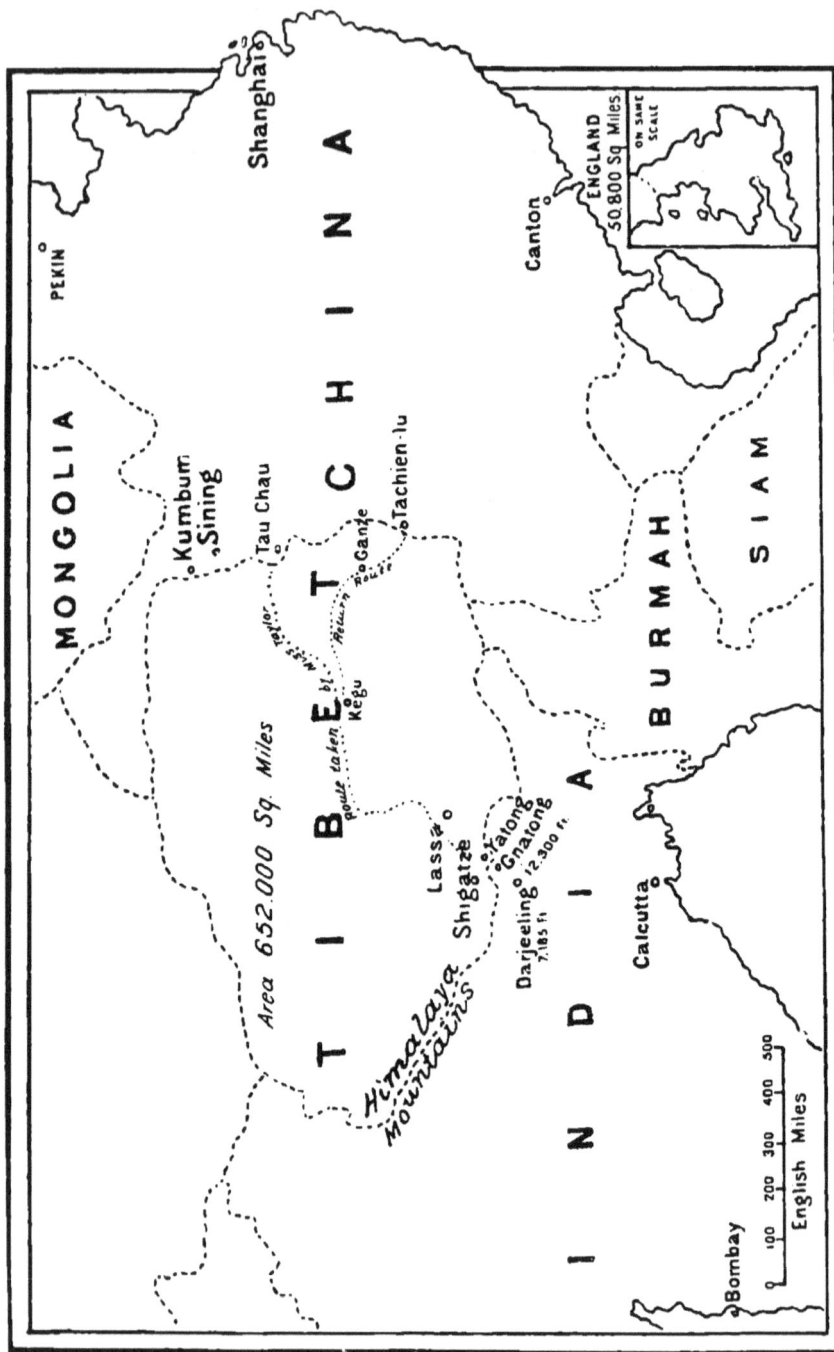

MONGOLIA

PEKIN

Shanghai

C H I N A

Canton

ENGLAND
50.800 Sq Miles

ON SAME
SCALE

Kumbum
Sining

Tau Chau

Tachien-lu

Ganze

T I B E T

Area 652.000 Sq. Miles

Kegu

Lassa

Shigatze

Yatong
Gnatong 12.300 ft

Darjeeling
7.185 ft

Himalaya
Mountains

I N D I A

BURMAH

S I A M

Calcutta

Bombay

English Miles

0   100   200   300   400   500

Mission   {Yatong 10.050 ft above the level of the Sea
Stations {Gnatong 12.300 ft   „   „   „   „   „

PIONEERING IN TIBET.

—✦·✦·✦·✦—

Some Facts about Tibet.

THE demand for some account of the Tibetan Pioneer Mission has necessitated this little compilation. It shows how the Lord, after leading me through many dangers and difficulties, has enabled not only myself but Miss B. Ferguson and Miss M. Mary Foster, to live and proclaim within the borders of Tibet (so long called "the closed land") the glorious gospel of salvation through Jesus Christ. While, however, the facts here recited will not be altogether new to some of my readers, it is felt that to many others they will be fresh, and their perusal necessary to a right understanding of the present position of an evangelistic effort, which, although in its infancy, has nevertheless not a little about it that is both remarkable and interesting.

The following sketch is reprinted from the pages of *The Christian* :—

Miss ANNIE R. TAYLOR,
Chinese Missionary and Traveller in Tibet.

"The heroism of faith finds fresh illustration in the remarkable journey accomplished by this young sister into the jealously-secluded regions of Tibet proper. Going in faith, believing that the Lord had sent her, she traversed thousands of miles where no European foot had ever trodden before. We are aware that certain travellers have crossed Tibet in various directions, but few indeed have penetrated Inner Tibet : and of those known to have reached Lhassa, only two have returned to tell the tale. Apart, however, from any question of priority, the journey just completed is of peculiar interest in that it was definitely undertaken by faith, and in order to open the way for the Gospel.

"Miss A. R. TAYLOR was early led to the knowledge of Jesus. Her thoughts were first directed to the heathen when a school girl at Richmond. Dr. Moffatt's son gave an address on Africa, which greatly impressed at least one of his young hearers. The place and power of women in missions had not then been discovered, and the whole drift of the speaker's appeal was for young men. His plea was, however, so forceful that the sympathetic young pupil almost wished she were a boy that she might go at once. From that time she read all the missionary literature she could obtain, and pondered the theme constantly. Some years later she found that the Lord wanted women for China, that they were being accepted and sent out by the China Inland Mission, and that their labours were being blessed in the Flowery Land. When very young she read in 'Near Home and Far Off' accounts of that strange mysterious region so rigidly closed against Europeans, and in this way Tibet seems to have laid hold of her mind.

"In due course Miss Taylor offered herself to and was accepted by the China Inland Mission. In 1884 she went out to China, and having learned the language, worked for a time in Tau-chau, near the Tibetan frontier. She was the first English person to reside in this city, and in 1887 visited the Great Lama monastery of Kum-bum, where the French priests, MM. Gabet and Huc, had previously learned Tibetan. Beyond this point no English traveller had gone, though a few Russians had explored the districts. That great unevangelised land pressed upon Miss Taylor's heart. When our Lord bade His witnesses 'go into all the world and preach the Gospel to every creature,' He knew all about Tibetan exclusiveness. 'We have,' she reflected, 'received no orders from the Lord that are impossible to be carried out.' In the story of the China Inland Mission, she saw how the great interior of China had seemed hermetically closed until the foot of faith pressed forward, and then strangely and wonderfully it opened before the Lord's servants as they went in to possess : so she believed it would be on 'the roof of the world,' as Tibet has frequently been termed by reason of its altitude. At length she resolved to make the attempt to penetrate Central Asia, and reach, if possible, Lhassa, the sacred city of the Lamas, and the capital of Tibet. This city lies nearer our Indian frontier than to China.

"Leaving China in 1888, Miss Taylor came home *via* Australia and India, and went on to Darjeeling, on the Bengal frontier, going to a Tibetan village near Darjeeling, her object being to learn the language. From there she pressed forward into Sikkim (not then under English rule). 'I went,' she says, 'in simple faith, believing that the Lord had called me. I knew that the difficulties were great, and that enemies would be numerous ; but I trusted God to take care of me, just as He protected David from the hands of Saul.' She got not far from Kambajong, a Tibetan fort. Here the natives would ask her frequently what they were to do with her body if she died. She told them she was not going to die just then. They have, however, a custom of 'praying people dead,' and to this they resorted, taking care to help their prayers in a very effective manner. One day the chief's wife invited the stranger to eat, and prepared rice and a mixture of eggs for her.

"Some conversation between the women as she was eating aroused Miss Taylor's suspicion as to the eggs placed before her ; and sure enough, after she had partaken, she became ill, with all the symptoms of aconite poisoning. The Tibetan chief was greatly alarmed at her living so near the border, and came over and ordered her back to Darjeeling. She refused to go there ; but settled down in a hut near a Tibetan monastery called Podang Gumpa, living as best she could.

"After a year spent in Sikkim, during ten months of which she never saw a European, being surrounded by natives only, Miss Taylor was led to see that it was the Lord's will she should enter Tibet by way of China. Her stay at Sikkim had, however, not been in vain. First, she had learned the language as spoken at Lhassa, and secondly she had secured a faithful Tibetan servant. This young man, Pontso, is a native of Lhassa. Travelling on the frontier of India he had hurt his feet, and was directed to the white stranger for treatment. He had never seen a foreigner before, and the kindness shown him won his heart ; so that from that time he has been her constant companion and devoted servant, as well as a follower of Jesus.

"Taking him with her, Miss Taylor sailed for Shanghai, went up the great river to Tauchau, a city in Kansuh, on the borders of Tibet, and surrounded by Tibetan villages. She visited several large monasteries, and became familiar with many phases of Tibetan life and character. In the monasteries she found some intelligent lamas, free from the grosser superstitions, and willing to lend her what assistance she required.

" A year was thus spent on the frontier, and at last came the longed-for opportunity of penetrating the interior. It came about thus. A Chinese Mohammedan, Noga, had a wife from Lhassa, and he had promised her mother that he would return to Lhassa with his wife in three years. This he wished to do ; but, having no money, he consented to conduct Miss Taylor to the capital, provided she found the necessary horses and funds. Mrs. Noga had already become very friendly with the young English lady, because she could speak her language, which the natives on the Chinese side could not do. Thus the way was prepared, and on September 2nd, 1892, Miss Taylor and her four servants, two Chinese and two Tibetans, started from Tau-chau for the interior.

" The country is one mass of lofty mountains, a large part of it is above the snow line ; the roads are merely mountain tracks, while the people seem to live almost wholly by brigandage, preying incessantly on the caravans which traverse the country. Hence the account of the long and arduous journey is simply a narrative of sore hardship amid snow and ice, perils from lawless robbers, and yet graver perils from her faithless and false guide, for Noga proved to be a great rascal, whose only object in taking Miss Taylor into Tibet appeared to be to rob and murder her : in the first he succeeded pretty thoroughly ; but in the second he failed, inasmuch as she had ' a shield of defence ' of which he dreamt not, and she was kept with a sure hand.

" Four days after leaving Tau-chau the little party encountered eight brigands, who were fortunately having tea, and took some time to light up the tinder-boxes of their match-locks. Miss Taylor's party had only five fighting-men ; but these, led by a young priest or lama, who was intensely fond of fighting, skilfully kept off the enemy until, after much firing but no bloodshed, they had to retreat. Three days after, a friendly caravan of Mongols was joined, which much increased the strength of the party. Soon after the entire caravan was surrounded by 200 brigands, firing on all hands. Resistance was useless, and most of the men slipped away, leaving the property to the enemy. Two men were killed and eight wounded, and seven horses and some yak wounded. At last the lama packed off the two women and Miss Taylor's faithful Tibetan servant, Pontso, calling out to the enemy that they were women. They were allowed to ride away, as it is against the Tibetan custom to fire at a woman. It appeared that this attack was a piece of retaliation, the Mongols composing the caravan having previously robbed the tribe now attacking them. To prevent their being followed, the assailants took the chief man among the prisoners as a hostage, to be killed if they were pursued. Miss Taylor was amused at the truthful answers returned on all points as to property and as to who was the chief man, but found that absolute truth-fulness is part of the etiquette of Tibetan tribal warfare. The people lie terribly in trade or social affairs, but in dealing with an enemy will not stoop to deception.

" Meanwhile Noga began, now that he was fairly in the heart of the mountains, to show his hand, and not only tried to strike and abuse Miss Taylor, but attempted again and again to murder her. Humanly speaking, she was only saved by the vigilance of her servant and the ready help of some native villagers and lamas. At length she had to leave Noga and his wife, and with her servant, Pontso, and another Tibetan named Patcgn, she pressed on, penniless and comfortless, for the capital. They had many tokens of the presence of God. At one time they lost their way for three days in the mountains, finding afterwards that this had been God's method of sheltering them from a deliberate attempt at murder planned by Noga. Foiled in these purposes, he spread the report that Miss Taylor had gold and precious stones round her body—this being done to tempt the cupidity of the natives to kill her for the booty. Then he went on to Lhassa and told the authorities of her coming. These sent out stringent orders that she must be stopped, but not injured. Thus, when three days' journey from Lhassa, she was arrested by soldiers and brought before an official, who told her that if she resolutely went on he could not stop her, but he would be executed for letting her pass. She would have no man's blood shed for her, and so—though on the verge of fulfilling her long-cherished idea—she turned back on a terrible return journey to China. The chiefs from Lhassa gave her two horses, an old tent, and some food, as her tents were gone, she being robbed by Noga of two horses, a tent, and nearly all the food ; but half-way back the food was finished, and the tent given away, Miss Taylor being misled by the Tibetans.

"Sometimes travelling was so dangerous on account of brigands that the escort dare not stop, and travelling went on day and night. On the way to Lhassa, Miss Taylor, with the greatest difficulty, induced them to stay while a tall, strong servant, a Chinese Mohammedan, lay dying of congestion of the lungs, calling pitiably to Allah to help.

"On the return journey another strong man, a Tibetan, died from the effect of the cold, and Miss Taylor herself at great altitudes had repeated attacks of palpitation. Cooking, when there was anything to cook, was most difficult, as the water boiled with so little heat. Frequently pieces of ice, put in to replenish the pan, floated in boiling

MISS ANNIE R. TAYLOR.

water some time before melting. Once she was twenty nights in the open air sleeping on the ground, snow falling all the time, as neither tent nor house was to be found. The horses were almost starved, the snow covering everything. The poor animals even ate woollen clothing when they got the chance. A small ration of cheese, mixed with tea and butter, was often all that could be spared for them. Having lost her money, Miss Taylor could not buy a goat. Raw goat's flesh is an emergency food for horses in Tibet, and they like it. In fact, owing to the absence of grass, Tibetan horses will eat almost anything. Crossing fords was a very tiresome task. At first they crossed on rafts made of inflated skins, with a few branches tied across. Later on, swimming on horseback was the only course, and this meant being up to the waist in water, the horse's head alone visible, and running the risk of tumbling into the torrent, and then on the slippery ice.

" A most remarkable experience was the meeting with the tribe known as the Goloks, governed by a woman chief named Wachu Bumo. This is a most ungovernable tribe, amenable neither to Chinese nor to Tibetan authority, and living entirely by plunder. They go out in irresistible parties of 500 to 2000, and are so certain of victory that the women and children go out to see the fun. Plunder seems to be profitable, for they are the wealthiest tribe in Tibet. Wachu Bumo took quite a fancy to Miss Taylor, and gave her a royal safeguard. Finally, after many adventures, which will be told in her forthcoming book, Miss Taylor reached Ta Chien Fu, in Chinese territory, on April 12th, having left the Lhassa district on January 22nd, the first English lady, and certainly the first messenger of the Gospel, to penetrate to the heart of Tibet.

" Many readers, profoundly concerned for the spread of
the Gospel, will ask what has all this to do with mission
work ?   Much, we reply.   As Livingstone by his great
journeys opened the way for the Gospel into dark Africa,
so our sister expects that God will use her journey to pave
the road for missionaries.   She believes that the promise
stands good : ' Every place that the sole of your foot shall
tread upon, that have I given unto you '; and in the name
of the Lord God she has taken possession of Tibet, fully
anticipating that as soon as the right men arise to go
forward and possess the land the way will be made plain,
and the Gospel be published in this hitherto inaccessible
region."

An Englishwoman in Tibet.

I HAD the pleasure of contributing the following article to *The National Review* of September, 1893. It is here reprinted by the kind permission of the Editor.

It was not until after various residences of some length, between the years 1887 and 1892, on the Indian and the Chinese frontiers of Tibet, during which I had freely mixed with Tibetans, at times worn their dress, and acquired a colloquial use of the language, that I felt fitted to penetrate the interior of the country. My stay on the Indian side had been specially fruitful. I had learnt the language as spoken at the capital, Lhassa (it is more of a dialect on the Chinese side). And it was on this border, when living in a hut among the Tibetans of Sikkim, that I came across my faithful little Tibetan man-servant, Pontso, now with me in England. A native of Lhassa, he had run away from a cruel master to take refuge in India, where he arrived in a pitiable condition. I was asked by some Tibetans to doctor him, and I brought him back to health and strength. He thus became attached to me, and entered my service, to accompany me in 1891, *viâ* Calcutta, to Shanghai, and thence the many weary miles through China till we again reached the Tibetan frontier.

Here I settled in the old city of Tau-chow, some miles from the modern town, in Kan-suh, the most north-western province of China, to await an opportunity of penetrating into Tibet proper. This opportunity came at last. Among my acquaintances in the old Chinese town I counted a Chinese Mohammedan, Noga by name, married to a Lhassa woman called Erminie. Noga had been to Lhassa several times, and on his last expedition had brought away Erminie, who was given him to wife by her mother for the term of three years. That time was now fully up, and Erminie was anxious to return home. They were accordingly thinking over the ways and means of the journey; and, knowing my desires, proposed that I should engage Noga as guide and head servant, and make the expedition with them. My idea was to pass through the capital, and, after some stay at Lhassa, to travel on across the Himalayan passes to Darjeeling, thus traversing the country and getting a general knowledge of the people. Noga agreed to conduct me the whole way; and we finally concluded a bargain by which he was to make all necessary preparations, receiving money from me for the expenses.

Among the several advantages which accrued to him, one was that the horses were to be his when the journey was over. I hoped this condition would induce him to buy good and hardy animals; but in this, as in many other things, I was soon to be undeceived. Much of my money, I afterwards found, he had pocketed or spent in purchases for his own use.

It was on the 2nd of September, 1892, that I set out on my long-wished-for journey. My party consisted of myself and five Asiatics—Noga, the Chinese Mohammedan guide and my head servant; Erminie, the Tibetan woman, Noga's wife till she reached her home at Lhassa; Leucotze, a young Chinese Mohammedan servant; Pontso, my faithful Tibetan, who had become a Christian; and Nobgey, a fellow-traveller, a Tibetan borderman bound for Lhassa. Our cavalcade numbered sixteen horses. Nobgey and Erminie rode their own; the other ten were mine, consisting of mounts for myself and three servants, and six pack-horses laden with our two tents, bedding, cloths for barter, presents for chiefs, and food for two months. The brigands relieved me of a good part of this luggage, together with two of my horses, a few days after crossing the border; while poor Nobgey was bereft of nearly all his belongings, and took a sad leave of us to retrace his steps to the Chinese border. Our road first lay through the district inhabited by the agricultural tribes on the frontier. Then we entered the country occupied by the Mongols of the Ko-ko Nor. The pasture there was the richest I have seen in any part of Tibet; but an idyllic pastoral life is by no means practised by the inhabitants. Brigandage is the general profession. The young men spend their time either in making raids on travellers and on the encampments of other tribes, by which means they mostly acquire their cherished horses, or in practising the art of warfare. I witnessed a military tourna-ment at which some riders at full gallop fired one after another at a small given mark.

These Mongols are tall and fierce-looking, though they proved amiable when friendly. The men shave their heads. Both men and women dress in a gown of sheep-skin girded round the waist, high boots of felt and skin, bound below the knee with a leathern strap or cotton garter, and long white felt coats, which they wear over the sheep-skins when it rains. Their summer hat is of white felt, in shape some-thing like the top hat worn by the old Welsh market-women; the cap they wear in winter is of white astrakan, shaped like a sugar-loaf, with a red and green cotton brim. The women dress their hair in little plaits, more than a hundred, caught together at the ends in a wide band of coloured cloth, which is embroidered with gay silks and gold thread, and studded with coral and turquoise, silver coins and brass buttons, which they get from Lhassa. The tents are round; the inner sides of trellis-work, the top of wooden ribs, giving an umbrella shape, and the whole covered with white felt, with an aperture for a small door of wood, and a hole in the roof to let out the smoke.

We left this district to enter one in comparison with the inhabitants of which the Mongols are very Arcadians. On the 28th of September we crossed the Yellow River (or Ma-chu), as the Tibetans call it, at its first bend westward, and came among the Golok tribes.

The country of this people extends from that point south-wards as far as a high range of mountains running from east to west, and is watered by the Yellow River. It is treeless and very hilly ; but the pasturage is fairly good in the valleys and on the lower slopes of the mountains, which even in September show a clearly marked snow-line. The Goloks are shorter and slighter in stature than the Mongols, and have higher cheek-bones and rounder faces. The men wear their hair long and hanging down to their shoulders ; their sheep-skins are drawn up by the girdle, forming a kind of kilt below the waist and a large pouch above, in which they always carry their wooden tea bowls, called po-pa, and many other things, when on a journey. The boots are of leather with skin soles and cloth leggings bound below the knee (which is left bare like a Scotch Highlander's) by a long woven garter of various bright-coloured wools. The hats, made of the fur of foxes, sheep-skins, or felt, are of many peculiar shapes. The dress of the women is like that of the men ; but the sheep-skin gowns reach to their ankles. Their hair is in two plaits, hanging down their backs, and enclosed at the ends in a sheath of cloth ornamented with round pieces of amber and cowrie shells, which they buy from the Chinese. Long earrings of silver and coral hang from both ears ; the men limit themselves to one very massive piece of jewellery in the right ear. The tents, utterly unlike those of the Mongols, are made of woven black cloth of the coarse hair of the yâk, the Tibetan ox. They are about forty feet by twenty, and are supported by one small beam on two poles inside and by several props outside. The ropes are made of the hair of the yâk's tail. These Golok tribes are the most notorious brigands in Tibet. They are feared both by travellers and by other nomadic people like themselves, and they acknowledge neither Tibetan nor Chinese sway. Pouring forth upon their preconcerted forays in numbers varying from five hundred to two thousand, they fall upon the tribes in the given district, and, surrounding them close on all sides, carry off, as booty, cattle, horses, sheep, tents, and fire-arms. They never fire upon the affrighted owners unless resistance is offered; but so sure are they of their prey that some of their women and children accompany them to enjoy the fun. It is not surprising that these people are the biggest cattle-owners in Tibet, a Golok chief being the happy possessor of a good ten thousand head. The tribes thus divested of their cattle and worldly goods sometimes rally to one leader, make an incursion into the Golok country, and continue by stratagem to get back some of their stolen property. They generally, however, prefer the easier way of retaliating upon innocent wayfarers; and by degrees get a small herd together again by lying in wait for caravans to and from Lhassa. Upon these they descend at night, and carry off the grazing yâk and horses to some secluded spot behind the hills, where they hide till the caravan is well on its way again. Thus, the Golok tribe of brigands are in a great measure responsible for the dangers and robberies to which travellers in Tibet are subject.

I had suffered much from loss of property when I was lucky enough to fall in with a Golok chieftainess. She gave me an escort of two Goloks when I left the country of the marauders, which was on the 19th of October. Shortly

PONTSO AND SIGJU.

afterwards my young Chinese servant, Leucotze, was taken very ill. The cold and exposure had been too much for him. Tibetan altitudes are great; and we had ridden in storms of rain and snow, and crossed rivers where there were no ferries or fords. Owing to the danger of the district, we were obliged to press on; but as the sick man grew worse and worse—he was suffering from pneumonia—I with difficulty induced the two Goloks to halt for a short time. The end was drawing near, and was accelerated by Noga, who insisted upon washing his body before death, Mohammedan fashion. We buried him at noon. A bright sun lighted up the snow-clad hills when the men dug up a few hard sods in some swampy ground close by, laid down the body in its shroud of white cotton cloth, and covered it as best they could with the frost-bound earth. At night the wolves were howling round the grave. This was in the Peigo country.

Next day we passed into the Sa-chu-ka country, the tribes of which also live by brigandage, though they are so far civilised as to pay taxes to China. The people were friendly, and exchanged two of my tired horses for fresh ones; but my party kept watch the whole of the night we spent in the native encampment. We were visited by A-tra, a Lhassa man, who had settled in this district and married a woman of the tribe; and he, Pontso, and Erminie, while keeping the night-watch, passed the time by relating wonderful stories and hairbreadth escapes, and droned out many a Tibetan ballad.

Leaving this district, our way led us through a more smiling landscape, past monasteries, villages, and fertile crops of barley, peas, and turnips. We stopped the night at a village hard by the Sha-i-Gumpa, and the next day came to the Dri-chu. This we crossed in a boat made of skins tightly stretched over a wooden frame. A steep ascent from the river's bank brought us to the picturesque

little town of Gala, whose houses rise one above the other
up the mountain. Here we made some stay in the home
of a Tibetan couple, Pa-tegn and Per-ma. The courtship
and marriage of this couple had been romantic. Pa-tegn,
when a baby, was set apart to become a lama. As a boy,
he lived at the Lamaserai (or monastery), where he learnt
to read and write, and did the duties of a priest. But,
when he was about twenty years of age, he fell in love with
Per-ma. Celibacy is a *sine quâ non* for lamas, and the chief
was shocked. One fine day, then, this Tibetan Abelard
disappeared, and in company with Per-ma made his way to
Lhassa. Here Pategn let his hair grow long, cast off his
priest's robe, and prosaically took to tailoring and boot-
making. On the birth of a girl they returned to Gala with
presents to pacify the chief, and settled down in their
native town. Their house, like most in the town, was built
into the hill ; the stables and cow-shed were on the ground
floor ; the first storey contained the kitchen and a small
sleeping-room, of which the roof formed the verandah for
the storey above. The second storey was the most
important. It contained a large open room to receive
guests and quarter travellers, and a small prophet's chamber
reserved for the lama when he came to read prayers for the
benefit of the family. In the roof above were stored the
grain and the straw, the latter serving as fodder during the
winter months. In looks the inhabitants of Gala bear a
strong resemblance to portraits of the time of Charles the
First. They have long, narrow faces, aquiline noses,
pointed chins, and big lips ; cut their hair in a fringe over
the forehead, and wear it hanging long—men and women
alike. Their gowns are of red or blue or white cloth,
woven at Lhassa. They drink freely of a spirit distilled
from barley, love singing and dancing, and, like most
Tibetans, are full of fun. Pategn, who was an experienced

traveller (having even reached Tau-chow, my starting place on these travels), journeyed on with me from Gala, replacing poor Leucotze in my service. Our route lay over the Rab-la, one of the most difficult passes in Tibet. We stopped a night at the village of Rab-da, and on the morrow we passed by Ma-ni-tang, a largish town for Tibet, on our way to the big and important town Ke-gu. We first caught sight of the Ke-gu Lamaserai beautifully situated on the top of a high rock at the foot of which lies the town.

Ke-gu, the half-way halting place on the famous tea road between the Chinese border town Ta-chien-lu and the Tibetan capital, is the centre of the tea trade, and accordingly the residence of numerous tea-merchants. It has many Chinese inhabitants, a mandarin from Si-ning, and a mandarin from Lan-chav. It is the Chinese who chiefly bring the tea here, to sell it to the Tibetan merchants, who forward it to Lhassa. The currency in this trade is the Indian rupee, which, however, is often dispensed with ; and then the tea is bartered by the Chinese for wool, hides, and furs, gold dust, mercury, and other Tibetan products, for importation into China. The tea (branches as well as leaves) is packed in pressed bricks about fourteen inches long, ten wide, and four thick. Eight of these bricks are sewn in a skin, and a yâk carries two skins. All Tibetans drink tea. They boil it, branches and all, in water with a little soda and salt, and before drinking add butter, barley flour (which is called tsampa), and dried native cheese. The solid part of this mixture when merely moistened with a little liquid tea and made up into hard balls is called ba, and forms the staple food of Tibet. The chief meat consumed is mutton, upon which the black tent people almost live. Sheep are cheap. In the interior of the country they cost from one rupee to two rupees. For winter consumption they are killed early in the cold season, and the meat is frozen.

Leaving Ke-gu after a lengthy stay, we followed the tea road as far as the Pau-gau Lamaserai. Here we quitted the highway for a mountainous route, which took us over the Pass O-may, till we reached Tash-e-Gumpa, which is situated on the river Tsa-chu. By this monastery we took up our quarters for twenty days in a cave excavated in the gravel of the hill-side ; and we were kindly treated by the chief lama, from whom we obtained a horse and some food in exchange for a few remaining English goods. Here the Chinaman Noga, who had behaved very badly the whole time, with his wife Erminie, left me, carrying off one of my horses, a mule, and the larger of my tents. I was not sorry to get rid of him ; for he had frequently threatened, and even attacked, my life. My party now consisted of myself and the two Tibetans Pontso and Pategn. Besides the horse obtained from the chief lama, we had three worn-out hacks left, two of which we exchanged for old beasts with little flesh on their bones. The remaining tent I was obliged to sell for bare necessaries : so from now, the 15th of December, we slept in the open air, choosing holes in the ground, that we might have a little shelter from the cold high winds. Joining a small caravan on the way to an encampment, we first followed a road through a valley thickly populated with nomads, and watered by the Tsa-chu, which we frequently crossed. After a march of seven days, we again struck the tea road, and, crossing the mountain-pass Tsa-nang-los-bu-la, came to the district Damchung, watered by the Long-chu. Having crossed this river, we traversed a small plain, and partly following the stream up its course, came to the Dam-jau-er-la, one of the highest and most dreaded Tibetan passes. The cold here is generally so intense that many travellers freeze by the wayside.

Stopping to attend the cold-stricken men would only mean destruction to the rest of the party. We came unscathed through this redoubtable pass to cross another, the Long-er-tsa-ke-la. The valleys here were populated thickly with the black tent tribes, who, judged by their large herds of cattle and horses, were evidently well-to-do.

We still marched, with slow pace and sorry exterior, along the tea road, which took us on over the So-ba-ner-la, and on the 28th of December across the Sok-chu, the river followed up by Captain Bower on his late expedition, till it brought us within sight at last of the boundary of our promised land—the waters of the Bo-Chu, which confine the Lhassa district, the sacred province of Ü. We were prepared for this: we had been meeting large caravans returning from the capital. On the last day of the old year (1892) we crossed the river and found ourselves within the sacred district.

Pategn told me that last year, when he travelled by, there were a troop of soldiers encamped there, on the look-out for a European traveller who (they had heard) was on his way to Lhassa. The Ü province is governed by the Lhassa lamas in the person of a chief appointed from the capital. On the side we entered, one chief rules over the district Na-chu-ka between the Bo-Chu and the confines of Leu-dring-tsong; which latter is under the sway of another head, the Pem-ba chief.

On the other side of the Bo-Chu the road took us over the Peh-la-me. We recrossed the river, passed by an encampment on the banks of a small lake called Ang-nga, and by a steep descent came to a deep gorge, through which flowed the Da-chu, which we crossed to pursue our way over a very stony course. At this point we were suddenly confronted by two fully-armed Tibetan soldiers, who bade us halt and informed us we were their prisoners.

We had perforce to stop, and, resigning ourselves to the situation, took up our position on the banks of a frozen stream hard by. This was on the 3rd of January. We were very soon surrounded by soldiers; but it was not until the evening, upon the arrival of a chief, that we learnt the reason of our detention. Noga had by making long stages arrived with the woman, some few days ago, at Na-chu-ko-kang. He had informed the resident chief that while on the road he had met two Tibetans conducting a European lady through the country. He had told them to take her back to China, which they had flatly refused to do: so, accordingly, at great inconvenience, he had hurried on to give information to the Government. He hinted his expectations of a reward; but the chief wished first to be assured the story was true. Then Noga regretted he must hurry on to Lhassa; but the chief, whose duty it was to send scouts in every direction (no joke in case of a hoax), refused to allow him to go till his information had been verified. The wily Chinaman was caught in his own trap.

In three days there arrived a military chief of some importance. His sheep-skin was trimmed with a wide band of bright blue lasting of European manufacture, and was bordered with a broad strip of beaver; but what specially drew my attention was the fantastic way in which his hair was dressed. The fringe across his forehead was caught together at the ends in a kind of horizontal Grecian plait not unlike the plaited edging of straw litters in a well-appointed stable; his back hair hung down in plaits which started from the crown of the head. Of his earrings, gold and coral, one was pendant, and the other a round piece of jewellery. His sword sheath was of massive silver, studded with coral and turquoise. As soon as his tent was pitched he sent for Pontso, and cross-questioned him about the foreign lady and himself. Then he invited me to his tent,

and asked me where I was going to, where I came from,
and whether I had made any maps.   He informed me that
he could not allow me to continue my journey; but he was
on the whole very friendly.   Both Pontso and Pategn were
strictly watched; and, after settling down for the night's
rest in the most comfortable hole to be found, were
surrounded all night by at least twenty soldiers.   I myself
was left unmolested in my narrow coffin-shaped hole.   I
had demanded that Noga and his wife should be brought
before me, that I might clear my servants of the charge
Noga had brought against them.   For this the presence of
a Lhassa chief was necessary; and, on the sixth day of our
detention, orders were given to set out, and we did a long
day's march towards Lhassa.   It was so cold that my limbs
grew stiff and numb, and I had to stop and get my servants
to collect some cattle dung (the Tibetan fuel) and light a
fire by the way.

When we arrived at our journey's end, they pitched a tent
for us.   We were close to the conjunction of the Si-ning
and the Tea road.   There are three roads to Lhassa—one
by Nag-chu-ko-kang, where custom is levied from all the tea
caravans, was situated on the other side of a hill close by.
For the levying of this custom, two Lhassa chiefs reside
permanently at Nag-chu-ko-kang; and both of them,
accompanied by a chief of lesser importance, came to
interview us, bringing Noga and Erminie with them.   As
soon as their tents were pitched, they sent for Pontso; and
they subsequently asked me to come before them.   As a
mat was not placed for me on which to sit, I sent for one;
and when they tried to browbeat me I refused to answer
impolite questions.   Noga at first denied all we said; but
upon his wife being cross-examined a little of the truth was
extracted.   During the trial, which lasted several days,
communication with Lhassa was kept up continuously.   A

youth who had been to Sikkim was sent to the encampment,
and proved the truth of Pontso entering my service there.
Word was sent from headquarters that I was to be treated
well; whereupon the chiefs treated me with respect. We
excited much curiosity; and Pontso was often invited in
the evening to the chiefs' tents, to entertain them by
accounts of the lives of the English, of what he had seen
in India, and the railways and steamships by which he had
travelled. They were also interested in my attempts; and
told me that of all later European travellers I had reached
the nearest to Lhassa, from which we were only a three-days'
ride. The ultimatum of the trial was that if I liked I could
go on to Lhassa. Should I do so, however, they, the
chiefs, having given me this permission, would lose their
lives, and my servants would be seized. I, as an Annia (a
woman religious teacher), would surely not wish to bring
about the death of innocent men? Should I, however,
decide to return to China, all necessities for our journey as
far back as Ke-gu, the half-way halt, would be given.

The true case of the matter was pretty obvious; but I
was not in a position to fly in the face of such persuasive
opposition. They gave me two extra horses, an old tent,
provisions, and ten ounces of silver in rupees and Tibetan
money. An escort of ten soldiers was to accompany us for
eleven stages; but a few days after we left the encampment,
which was on the 18th of January, we overtook a yâk
caravan, on which our escort quitted us. The progress of
this caravan was too slow for us. We went on ahead, to
arrive on the 2nd of February at Tash-e-gumpa, where we
had lived in the gravel cave from the 26th of November till
the 15th of December.

Fortunately, we pitched our tent on the side of the river
opposite to that of the monastery. Crowds of hostile-
looking lamas collected on the banks to watch us. The

chief who had been friendly to us was away; but the head lama in charge told Pategn on the morrow that Erminie, before she and Noga had abandoned us, had spread the report that I was a witch, could see through mountains and inside all the temples, and took note of all the gold and silver in the mountains. On our re-arrival, therefore, the lamas wanted to stone myself and my servants and throw our bodies into the river. This the head priest prevented them from doing; arguing that, as the chief at Nag-chu-ka had given me a tent and two horses, I could not be what Erminie represented.

From here our difficulties were much increased by the great depth of the snow. Three of our horses succumbed, for the grass was scanty and hard to procure. As the yâk caravan caught us up, we continued with it till we reached Ke-gu, which was on the 21st of February. Here Pategn left us to return to his home at Ga-la; for I no longer intended to retrace my steps, thinking it best to continue along the Tea road to Ta-chien-lu, and, once in China, to travel up the Yang-tse river to Shanghai. I gave him, in part payment for his services, two of the remaining three horses and the tent (which, I was told, I should no longer require). My last horse was spirited away, and we found ourselves in a predicament. The two Chinese officials were changing; the old ones had left for China, and their successors were not yet arrived; the lama chiefs told us we must not stay; the people refused to sell us horses. We finally came to terms with some O-gan-ze men returning to their native town. They were to lend us two horses for the journey, and to provide food and lodging for the night in rest houses, for a certain sum of money, which they wanted paid down. They were not particular as to keeping their word. Instead of stopping at the rest houses, they encamped in the open for the sake of economy, piling up the packs to

c

the weather side for shelter. The day after leaving Ke-gu we passed the boundary line between Amdo and Kham on a mountain, and stayed a night at Kar-sa, where tea-merchants reside. This town, like all others in Kham, is nominally under the rule of the Chinese officials of Si-chuen, whereas Amdo is governed by Si-ning. We crossed the Dri-chu (Yang-tse-kiang), on the ice, which was not too strong, and made for the mountain pass of Mo-ro-la, near the summit of which we had to spend the night. The cold was so intense that one of the horses was found frozen in the morning. It had snowed nearly every night.

On entering the Kong-pa-sa-ga we put up at a good-sized inn. The people seemed well-to-do. The country is fertile, and pigs and fowls are plentiful—the first we had seen since we left the Chinese border. We passed on by Kor-ta-ge-gumpa, which is walled round. The houses are built of clay or bricks or stone, as far as the first storey, which is of wood; the pretty little trellis-work windows are lined with coloured tissue paper. Here there is a huge prayer-wheel. The benefit of the prayers wafted around is shared by the men who grind them out. After crossing the Tza-chu we arrived at O-gan-ze, whither the men had undertaken to bring us. It is a large town, the residence of a Chinese official, a Tibetan chief, and merchants. On the night of our arrival one of the men, one who had been troubled with numbed knees from the great cold, especially on the mountain passes, was taken ill and died—just able to see his wife and family. That I should have survived the exposure of this journey, to which two strong men had succumbed, was indeed marvellous.

I stayed a few days, and was much struck by the inhabitants. The men are tall and broad, with round faces, high cheek-bones, short noses, and Chinese eyes. They cut their hair in a fringe in front, and, that they may have a plait reaching to the ground, add a quantity of false hair to the back. In this they insert two or three ivory rings; then they catch it up and wind it round the head in the guise of a turban. The women dress their hair in tiny plaits—I counted one hundred and thirty-eight on one head—and wear gowns of wool or cotton cloth, white or red or blue. Their jewellery, in which they delight, is of silver and coral and turquoises. These O-gan-ze men make their livelihood as carriers between Ta-chien-lu and Ke-gu, and for this purpose keep horses and mules. The price of a pack-horse to cover this distance is ten or twelve rupees. They consider they have the monopoly, and attack men from other parts of the country who venture along their road.

Leaving O-gan-ze, we passed Da-tong, on the river Kon-sa, and the town of Oh-trang-go, where there are many Tibetan shop-keepers and a colony of five hundred Chinese. After Sau-ri-gumpa, an important place, we next reached Kham-ga-dak, where the temple is roofed with sheets of gold. A small house was pointed out to us as the birthplace of a former Buddha of Lhassa. Our road now made a deep descent and led us through beautiful forests. In these the province of Kham abounds; villages and monasteries are scattered about the hillsides; and the ground is tilled by the inhabitants—a pleasing contrast to the grass lands of Amdo, where the people mostly are nomadic. On the top of the Ya-ra-la we passed a small lake, so deep that it had never been fathomed, in which (we were told) a horse lived.

My Tibetan trip was now drawing to a close, and in a few days we arrived at the town of Ta-chien-lu, in the Chinese province of Si-chuen. This was on the 12th of April, 1893, seven months and ten days since I had set out from the Chinese town Tau-chow, in the province Kan-suh.

MISS TAYLOR READING TO PONTSO AND SIGJU.

My Experiences in Tibet.

WAS privileged some time since to read the following paper at Meetings of the Royal Scottish Geographical Society in Edinburgh and Glasgow.

In addressing the members of a learned Society, as I have the honour and pleasure of doing this afternoon, I feel much regret that, owing to my lack of scientific knowledge and the want of instruments, I was unable, during my late journey through Tibet, to make any of those observations which I know are valued by such a body. Tibet is, however, so little known, and information so scarce regarding its accessibility by travellers, that I feel that a short relation of my experiences, and a statement of facts, the knowledge of which I reaped in my late journey in that country and during my residence at various times on its frontiers, will not be uninteresting. I will deal especially with Eastern Tibet, of which I have the most experience.

There are three high-roads from the Chinese borders to the Tibetan capital, Lhassa. Two start at the south-east of Tibet, from Ta-chien-lu, the border-town in the Chinese province of Sze-chuen. Of these one is the official, or Ba-li-tang-Lam (*lam* is Tibetan for road), and is used by the Mandarins, and by official couriers; the other is the Tea Road or Ga-Lam, the route of the tea caravans. The third high-road starts from Si-ning (north-east of Tibet) in the Chinese province of Kan-su, and is called the Si-ning Lam. In the centre of the Nag-chu-ka district of Tibet

EARLY MORNING.

Miss Taylor visiting Encampment in the Mountains of Gnatong.
Mission Hut in the distance.

proper, and but a few days' journey from Lhassa, the Si-ning
Road converges into the Tea Road.

Of these three routes the official is the shortest. Another
advantage it has consists in the rest-houses at intervals by
the roadside, where travellers can stay, and fresh horses be
hired.   It is, however, the most mountainous of the roads,
and consequently the most expensive to travel by.   Nor
is it freer from marauders and robbers than any other
road.

The Tea Road traverses a country dotted over with
numerous villages, and has rest-houses at intervals of long
stages, as far as the town of Ke-gu, the centre of the tea
trade, and the half-way halting-place between the Chinese
frontier and the Tibetan capital.   From Ke-gu onwards
there are on either side of the Tea Road numerous black-tent

encampments, at which meat can be bought and tired-out horses exchanged for fresh ones. In the early part of the year mules can be hired for travelling by this route, but they are generally only taken as far as Ke-gu, at a hire of ten to twelve rupees each for the journey. Thence to Lhassa : the Tibetan ox, or yâk, the *Bos gruniens*, is employed, at the hire of four bricks of tea the animal. The conditions upon hiring yâk are : that if they die on the road, or are carried off by brigands other than the Golok tribes, the hirer bears the loss. With regard to the formidable Golok tribes just referred to, their attacks are so irresistible, that if they are the marauders, the hirer of the yâk need not make good the loss—the merchant loses his merchandise, the *drog-pa* his yâk. Should, however, the *drog-pa* (or cattle-owner) accompany the travellers, he has to be kept during the journey ; but, on the other hand, no compensation is made for animals dying or lost on the road. The Tea Road is not difficult to travel along, comparatively speaking. Although the mountains are high, their ascent and descent are mostly gradual. The water supply is plentiful, but the grass is in some places very scarce, by reason of the large herds of cattle, belonging to the black-tent settlements before referred to, which graze by the roadside.

The Si-ning Road, the direction of which, as you see, is south-west, passes for the most part through uninhabited country. The pasturage is good, but water at times is scarce. This is the least mountainous of all the roads.

From every town on the Chinese borders a road starts to Lhassa, but they all eventually merge into one of the three high-roads above mentioned. I set out in my late journey from the town of Tao-chow, known to the Tibetans as Wa-tze, on the Chinese borders of the province of Kan-su, by a road, which, after a few days' journey, joins the road running between the huge monastery La-ber-long (Tibetan name, Am-do Ta-shi gumpa)—to which are attached five thousand lamas—and the important town of Ke-gu.

Tao-chow lies some little distance from the river Tao, and the old city, at which I lived, is the centre of trade with Tibet and that part of Kan-su. This district is separated from Tibet by a range of hills, traversable by three passes, at which there are gates, guarded by Chinese soldiers, where custom dues are levied.

Between the years 1887–1892 I had made sojourns of some length on the Tibetan borders, two on the Indian frontier, two on the Chinese. My last stay on the Indian side had been especially fruitful, for I had learnt the language as spoken at Lhassa. And it was on this border, when living in a hut among the Tibetans of Sikkim, that I came across my faithful little Tibetan man-servant, Pontso, now with me. A native of Lhassa, he had run away from a cruel master to take refuge in India, where he arrived in a pitiable condition. He was sent by some Tibetan neighbours to me to doctor him, and, with the blessing of God, I brought him back to health and strength. Becoming attached to me on this account, he entered my service, to accompany me, in 1891, *via* Calcutta to Shanghai, and thence for many long miles through China, till we again reached the Tibetan frontier. Here I settled in the old city of Tao-chow (there is a modern Tao-chow a few miles off) to await an opportunity of penetrating into the interior of Tibet. This opportunity came at last.

Among my acquaintances in the old Chinese town I counted a Chinese Mohammedan, Noga by name, married to a Lhassa woman called Erminie. Noga had been to Lhassa several times, and on his last expedition had brought away Erminie, who was given him to wife by her mother for the term of three years. That time was now fully up, and Erminie was anxious to return home. They were accordingly thinking over ways and means of making the journey, and, knowing my desires, proposed that I should engage Noga as guide and head servant, and accompany them on the expedition. My idea was to make some stay at the capital, and thence to travel on across the Himalayan passes to Darjeeling, thus traversing the country and getting a general knowledge of the people, with a view to prepare the way for mission work. Noga agreed to conduct me the whole way; and we finally concluded a bargain by which he was to make all necessary preparations, receiving money from me for the expenses.

It was on the 2nd of September, 1892, that I set out on my long-wished-for journey. My party consisted of myself and five Asiatics: Noga, the Chinese Mohammedan guide and my head servant; Erminie, the Tibetan woman,

TIBETAN WANDERING MUSICIANS.

Noga's wife, who was to travel with us as far as Lhassa ;
Leucotze, a young Chinese Mohammedan servant ; Pontso,
my faithful Tibetan, who had become a Christian ; and
Nobgey, a fellow-traveller, a Tibetan borderman, bound
for Lhassa.   Our cavalcade numbered sixteen horses :
Nobgey and Erminie rode their own ; the others were mine,
and consisted of mounts for myself and three servants, and
of six pack-horses, laden with our two tents, bedding, cloths
for barter, presents for chiefs, and food for two months.
The brigands relieved me of a good part of this luggage,
together with two of my horses, a few days after crossing
the border ; while poor Nobgey was bereft of nearly all his
belongings, and took a sad leave of us, to retrace his steps
to the Chinese border.

Our road lay at first through the district inhabited by the
agricultural tribes on the frontier.   Fertile fields, populous
villages, temples surrounded by trees, met our eyes ; while
the picturesque natives in their bright cotton jackets and
sheepskin gowns, bordered with cloths of various colours—
with their smiling faces and animated looks, singing or
chatting while working in the fields, struck me by the vivid
contrast to the sober looks and apathetic appearance of the
Chinese on the other side.

But the country inhabited by the Drog-pa, or black-tent,
people is soon reached ; and here the aspect of the country
changes.   At first shrubs are to be seen ; but these gra-
dually disappear, and the country becomes a cheerless
waste.   These Drog-pa are divided into various tribes ; and
the tribes into numerous encampments.   A head chief is
acknowledged by the tribe ; while a minor one rules over
each encampment.   The Mongol tribes who have settled
in this district—namely, the Koko-Nor, between whom and
their Tibetan neighbours there is continual strife—speak
the Mongolian as well as the Tibetan languages.   On

account of their pillaging propensities, they are forbidden to cross the Chinese border ; but Chinese merchants come to them. They prefer, however, to trade with the lamas of the monastery of La-ber-long. The Mongol women embroider artistically with gold thread and coloured silks. They also make eye-protectors of horse-hair, worn by the natives as a protection against snow-blindness ; and manufacture large quantities of felt. This they use for tents, as also for rain-cloaks and other coverings. Their tents are different from those of the Tibetans ; their dress and mode of life are very similar. The women milk, churn, and tend the young cattle ; the boys and old men watch the flocks and herds. The young men spend their time in practising the arts of warfare, in waylaying and attacking travellers, and in fighting other tribes in the surrounding country. The Upper Yellow River, or Ma-chu, forms the boundary of the district inhabited by this people. This river we crossed on a pontoon, made by four inflated bullock-skins—one at each corner of a hurdle-like raft of interwoven branches. This was pulled across the river by two horses swimming, guided by two men, who floated on the water with a foot on the hurdle.

The Golok people on the other side of the river are very different from the Mongols in appearance, but much the same in their love of plunder and pillage. Gold is to be found in this district, both in the mountains and in the sands of the rivers ; but brigandage is the chief occupation. Nevertheless, I was hospitably entertained in their settlements—notably by a Golok chieftainess, who, upon my leaving their country, gave me an escort of two men to accompany me into a safer region.

We next came into the Sa-chu-ka country, which is rocky and stony. The tribes here also live by brigandage, though they are so far civilized as to pay taxes to China. Then we reached the monastery Sha-e-gumpa, and traversed a more smiling landscape, past monasteries, villages, and fertile crops of barley, peas, and turnips. The Tibetan monasteries that I saw did not consist, like the European, of one or more huge blocks of buildings ; but, on the contrary, of many small gaily-painted houses of various shapes, grouped round the big square temple. Sha-e-gumpa, situated high on a hill, was a most fantastic conglomeration of odd shapes and many bright colours. The next day we crossed the Di-chu (the Yang-tse-Kiang of China) and came to the picturesque little town of Gala, built, like most Tibetan towns, into the side of the hill. In the summer-time the Chinese find their way here to buy the gold washed by the Tibetans from the sand of the river. These latter exchange it for fifteen times its weight of not very pure silver ; while the buyers get eighteen times its weight on Chinese soil. The rocks at Gala are of a peculiar green shade, indicating the presence of copper. In appearance the inhabitants of Gala bear a strong resemblance to portraits of the time of Charles the First. They have long, narrow faces, aquiline noses, pointed chins, and big lips ; cut their hair in a fringe over the forehead, and wear it in long locks—men and women alike. Their gowns are of red, blue, or white cloth, woven at Lhassa. They drink freely of a spirit distilled from barley ; love singing and dancing ; and, like most Tibetans, are full of fun. Our Tibetan host, by name Pategn, with whose wife and little children I became very intimate, consented to join my little train, to replace Leucotze, my young Chinese Mohammedan servant, who had died from exposure as we were leaving the Golok country.

We next crossed the Rab-la, one of the most formidable passes of Tibet, and leaving behind us the large town, Ma-ni-tang, we came to the town Ke-gu, the half-way halting-place on the Tea Road, and the centre of the tea trade. This town is the residence of numerous tea-merchants, whose interests are guarded by a mandarin from Si-ning and another from Lan-chow. It is the Chinese who chiefly bring the tea here, to sell it to the Tibetan merchants, who forward it to Lhassa. The currency in this trade is the Indian rupee, which, however, is often dispensed with, and then the tea is bartered by the Chinese for wool, hides, and furs, gold dust, mercury, and other Tibetan products, for importation into China. The tea, branches as well as leaves, is packed in compressed bricks, about fourteen inches long, ten wide, and four thick. This tea is literally the sweepings of the plantations, and the dried leaves and branches of other plants are mixed with it. Eight

LHASSA WOMAN AND SON.
(Formerly Landlady of Mission Hut at Gnatong.)

of these bricks are sewed in a skin, and a yâk carries two skins. All Tibetans drink tea. They boil it, branches and all, in water, with a little soda and salt, and before drinking add butter, barley flour (which is called *tsampa*), and dried native cheese. The solid part of this mixture, when merely moistened with a little liquid tea and made into hard balls, is called *ba*, and forms the staple food of Tibet. The chief meat consumed is mutton, upon which the black-tent people almost live. Sheep are cheap. In the interior of the country they cost from one rupee to two rupees. For winter consumption they are killed early in the cold season, and are frozen.

Turning our backs on Ke-gu, we followed the Tea Road through the midst of numerous nomad tribes. These do not follow the freebooting profession, but are adepts at the less honourable one of petty thieving (these are Tibetan sentiments!). Mercury is found in this district. It is called by the Tibetans white earth poison, and is one of the exports to China. Salt and mineral soda are also to be obtained, and find ready sale at Lhassa and other parts of Tibet, being important items in Tibetan tea-making.

We left the high or Tea Road at the Pangan monastery for a mountainous route, which brought us to Tash-e-gumpa (*gumpa* = monastery), which is situated on the river Tsa-chu, and is the half-way halt between Ke-gu and Lhassa. We then continued our way along the valley of the river Tsa-chu. Here volcanic energy had evidently been at work. The variegated soil—red, pink, grey, brown, and white—was a novel sight. I especially admired the red earth, which cast a pretty pink glow on the sheep and horses grazing by the roadside. We passed a mineral spring, which threw a jet a foot above the ground. Our horses, though very thirsty, the rivers being frozen over, would not touch the waters from this spring, for they were bitter.

Upon crossing the Dam-jan-er-la, one of the most dreaded passes (though its ascent is gradual), we reached a greater elevation than any we had yet surmounted. The cold here is generally so intense that travellers often freeze by the wayside. Stopping to attend frost-bitten men would only mean destruction to the rest of the party. Breathing was very difficult, and I awoke in the night gasping for breath. I also suffered much from palpitation of the heart. It is probably known to you that the average elevation of Great Tibet is some 15,000 feet (the greatest altitude in the world, Mount Everest, is 29,000 feet). I was unable to make any scientific observations beyond noticing that on this pass our water boiled at so low a point that it was little more than tepid. We had to drink our tea very quickly to prevent a crust of ice forming on the top. And we took good care to touch no steel or iron for the sake of our epidermis. We came unscathed through this redoubtable pass, and crossed the Long-er-tsa-ke-la. On our descent we found the valleys thickly populated with the black-tent tribes, rich in large herds of cattle and horses.

We still marched on with slow pace and sorry exterior along the Tea Road, which took us on over the So-ba-ner-la, and on the 28th of December across the Sok-chu, the river followed by Captain Bower on his late expedition, till we came at last within sight of the boundary of our promised land, the waters of the Bo-chu, which here separate the province of Amdo from the sacred province of Ü. We were prepared for this, for we had been meeting large caravans returning from the capital. On the last day of the old year (1892) we crossed the river, and found ourselves within the Lhassa district.

Had I been strong enough, it would have been wise to have left our horses here, and continued the journey on foot, following up the course of the frozen river, as it winds in and out among the mountains, until we had reached a point near Lhassa. The natives say that this is some-times done. But the road is long, and the tribes dwelling on the banks of the river share the freebooting propensities of the eastern tribes: I therefore resolved to follow the usual route. After twice crossing the river, and passing a small lake called Ang-nga, our horses picked their way over a very stony course and down a steep descent till we came to the Da-chu, flowing through a deep gorge. Two days after crossing this river I was taken prisoner, to be con-ducted later on by military escort a very long day's journey nearer to Lhassa, within an hour or so of Nag-chu-ko-kang.

I was then within three stages of Lhassa, and at the junction of the Si-ning and the Tea Roads.

After much palavering with the Lhassa chiefs who came to interview me, I finally had to give up Lhassa for this time, and with my Tibetan servants, Pontso and Pategn, set out on my return journey to Ke-gu, varying the route by not always keeping to the high road.

After a long stay at Ke-gu, where I mixed much with the natives, we started for China in a south-easterly direction, with some muledrivers returning to Oganze, which is on the Tea Road, half-way to Ta-chien-lu. We soon entered the province of Kham, which with Amdo are the two principal Tibetan provinces that pay tribute to China. The taxes and customs levied in Ü are paid to the royal lama at Lhassa. But it were a difficult task to detail the relation of the various parts of Tibet, either to the Tibetan or the Chinese Government; still more to define exactly the nature of this relationship. We passed numerous small towns and villages, and the country, though mountainous, is, unlike the other mountainous districts we had traversed, well wooded and with occasional fertile districts. Hot sulphur springs abound as well as other springs of mineral waters, much valued by the Tibetans for their medicinal properties. I saw rocks of slate; and coal is found in abundance. It is used by the natives as fuel, but is not in great demand until the Chinese border is reached.

My Tibetan trip was now drawing to a close, and on the 12th of April, 1893, I arrived at the town of Ta-chien-lu, in the Chinese province of Sze-chuen.

This journey, which lasted seven months and ten days from the date I left Tao-chow in Kan-su to my arrival in Ta-chien-lu, cost me about £100, including the value of everything—horses, luggage, and provisions—stolen on the way. The vicissitudes of my property, owing to the attack of the brigands, and the brigand-like propensities of my ostensible guide and guardian, the Chinaman Noga, are too many to be enumerated. Suffice it to say, my cavalcade and luggage diminished visibly and grew beautifully less day by day. Noga, after several attempts upon my life, abandoned me (to my great relief) at Tash-e-gumpa, taking with him his wife Erminie and the greater part of my belongings.

Hurrying after us by double stages, and passing us when out of sight behind some hills, he carried information to the Lhassa chiefs about the foreign lady-traveller, and it is to him I owe my failure in reaching Lhassa and carrying out my idea of journeying thence over the Himalayan passes to Darjeeling. I was, when arrested in the Lhassa district, so destitute of money, and even of the necessities of life, that the Lhassa chiefs gave me the wherewithal to retrace my steps to the half-way town Ke-gu, where I had to leave my tents; and then for many a night I slept in the open air. My bed was either on the ground in the lee of a pile of luggage, or, if I chanced to find one, a hole, the sides of which protected me from the fierce icy blasts which blow over these great altitudes. A piece of felt to cover the ice at the bottom of the hole made my couch, and a warm sleeping bag into which I crept formed my sleeping clothes. Caves now and then proved a welcome luxury. I was in Tibetan dress, but this was only to avoid the gaze of too curious eyes. With regard to my servants, Noga, as you have heard, proved faithless; Leucotze, the other Chinaman, died; the two Tibetans—my faithful Pontso, and Pategn, who entered my service at Gala— alone stuck to me through thick and thin. The latter, Pategn, took leave of me upon our return to Ke-gu, and wended his way northwards to his home and wife and children at Gala. Pontso has never left me.

D

I have nothing but praise to give the Tibetans for their chivalry and kindness. Setting aside their raiding proclivities (of which, after all, in earlier times, we have had lively examples on our own borders), they are hospitable, friendly, trustworthy, and by no means averse to intercourse with Europeans. In simplicity, and naïveness more especially those people form a striking contrast to most Asiatic races. Although the lamas, for political reasons, do not wish to see us in their country, it is the Chinese who force Tibet, though this country is only partly tributary to them, to so jealously guard her frontiers; and this principally for their own trade interests; nor do they hesitate to do all they can to impede any intercourse between the Tibetans and Europeans, and to raise bad blood.

Should I be asked my opinion as to what is of most importance to Tibetan travellers, I should emphasise the necessity of the Tibetan language being mastered by all intending explorers; one is so peculiarly liable to be misled and deceived by Eastern interpreters. As this tongue is much easier to acquire than most Oriental languages, as for instance, Arabic or Chinese, it is not too formidable a task.

I shall trespass on your time for a little longer in order to reply to a frequent question regarding what I saw of the fauna and flora of Tibet. The following animals actually came under my personal observation :—

The yâk (*Bos gruniens*), both tame and in herds of wild ones. This curious black-coated and maned animal, in some points like a buffalo, in others like a horse, but which, clumsy as it looks, climbs precipitous ascents with a truly astonishing ease and celerity, and which grunts like a pig, has often been described. Not so an animal of the horse tribe, herds of which I came across on the lofty mountain ranges. This animal strongly resembles the quagga of

South Africa. It is shaped like a zebra, but with a stripe-less fawn-coloured coat, of a paler shade on the belly, and is, so the natives told me, untameable. One whole day's journey through snow-drifts and over snow-covered holes my little party safely followed in the wake of a herd of these animals, so unerring was their instinct in finding a safe footpath. Herds of deer were countless. We also came across flocks of wild sheep and goats, wolves, foxes, hares, marmots, and rats devastating whole acres. Among birds, the black and white eagles and the beautiful golden eagle were conspicuous. Vultures were innumerable, and play an economic part in the consumption of dead bodies, which are cut up in small pieces for their repast, the Tibetans objecting, from a feeling of sentiment, to the bodies of their friends being torn to pieces by the birds. Huge, impertinent, thievish crows would attack our provisions on the very backs of our pack-horses. Teal, and a little bird called *Tit* in Tibetan, were common.

When speaking of the flora I must remind you that a snow-covered ground does not offer much temptation to botanise. Except in Kham and on the borders, trees were conspicuous by their absence. A few fir stumps, juniper bushes, briers overhung with snow, and a sweet edible root given me by some natives claimed my attention in the interior. Edelweiss and other Alpine flowers grew on the borders.

Extracts from Letters.

Gnatong, 1895.

Y work at present lies chiefly amongst the numerous parties of Tibetans that nearly every evening, for seven months in the year, encamp here on the mountain sides. Gnatong is situated on the high trade-road to and from Tibet, for wool and other produce. Every evening there are from four to fourteen fresh encampments, with an average of six Tibetans to each camp. I go out and bid them welcome, and they invite me to sit with them around the fires, which I do ; and then after giving each of them one of Mrs. Grimke's text-cards, I tell them the old, old story of Jesus and His love for poor lost sinners.

They generally listen most attentively, and as they come from all parts of Tibet with the wool, the message is carried on far and wide into Tibet. I have given nearly three thousand of Mrs. Grimke's texts, and they are much appreciated. But the more thoughtful of them want something more. One man, a lama, said to me lately, when I gave him a card with John xvii. 3, "*Life eternal* means so much, I want to know more about it ; can you not give me a book ? " So I gave him a copy of one of the Gospels ; for through the kindness of Mrs. Robertson, Honorary Secretary of the Association for the Free Distribution of the Scriptures, I have been able to give away over five hundred copies of the Gospels in Tibetan, which I hear are being read by the lamas in various monasteries, even at Lhassa.

There is now a great demand for them, and I frequently get requests brought by the merchants from chiefs over the border to send them one of the Gospels in Tibetan. Thus making friends with the Tibetans and distributing God's Word in their midst is all helping on the cause we have at heart. In the summer months, when the wool trade ceases, the Tibetans of Sikkim bring up from the valleys their herds and flocks for pasture, and so we shall ever have fresh numbers amongst whom to spread the Gospel.

There is also work to do amongst the British troops stationed here. Some of the men come down every evening. On Sunday and Thursday I have Gospel Meetings, on Tuesday a Bible Reading, and on Saturday a Prayer Meeting. The Lord is blessing the word, and some of the men have decided for Christ.

Mr. John T. Collier—who as a lance-corporal of the Manchester Regiment was stationed at Gnatong, and whilst there, received Jesus as his Saviour, and became my right-hand helper in the work amongst the soldiers then stationed there—has now left the army and is accepted by Dr. H. Guinness as a Missionary student. He is studying at Cliff College, Curbar, Derbyshire, and when his course is completed is expecting to join the Tibetan Pioneer Mission. He writes, " I do hope that the Lord will help me in my studies, for I feel my utter need and dependence upon Him ; of myself I can do nothing, but through Christ Jesus who strengtheneth me I can rise victorious over all things."

December 31st, 1896.

Since my first arrival here we have distributed about one thousand copies of the Gospels in Tibetan, as well

as many in Chinese. These have been scattered far and
wide in Tibet.

On Christmas Day we had over two hundred Tibetans
and Chinese to tea, cake, bread and jam. No sooner
were our guests seated on the floor of a shed lent us for
the occasion, and I was standing up to give thanks, when
the floor gave way, and we went down about three feet.
Praise the Lord, no one was hurt, and only a few frightened.
Then part of our guests had tea in another shed, and part
in the open air—which we did not find too cold, as we are
used to the frost. After tea the tree was lighted, and
owing to the kindness of friends in England we were able
to give gifts to all who came. Some warm woollen cuffs
were much appreciated, but the dolls were the most sought
after. All wanted them, the chiefs and men and boys as
well as the women and girls. We gave one each to the
chiefs present, and it was most amusing to see them
nursing their coveted gift as they took possession of it.
Only having a few dolls, it was difficult to decide who
were to get them. After the tree we had the lantern, one
of the lamas present who stood just behind me as I
showed it, was much interested in the picture of "Christ
on the Cross," and asked me if He was not a great sinner,
and listened with wonder as I told them that Jesus, God's
Son, who had no sin, took the sinner's place and bore the
punishment due to our sins.

In conclusion we sang " Jesus loves me " in Tibetan,
which we have printed on a slide. We rejoiced that some
of the Tibetans should have a gift on the Anniversary of
the Birth of our Lord ; but oh, how we long for them to
know Jesus as their Saviour, and thus receive the gift of
Eternal Life ! Some of our guests came from the villages
lower down the valley, Rinchingong, Galling, Chumbi,
Gallingka, and Pepetang. A few came from the black

tents on the mountain side. The lamas were from the monasteries near by. Many of the women belong to Lhassa, their husbands being Chinese, and the Tibetan soldiers here now are from Shigatze. I think that the tree and lantern were new to all except those present last year, and one the year before at Gnatong. Mr. H. E. Hobson, a Commissioner of the Chinese Imperial Customs, the only European residing here, kindly helped us with the tree.

Patung, or Patong.

UR home in Tibet is situated in the Chumbi valley, and is a few miles over the Tibetan border. It was at one time governed by local chiefs subject to the Lhassa Government; but now there is a resident Tibetan chief, and the "Mart" is directly under the Lhassa rule. We pay the rent of the mission premises to him, and he forwards it to Lhassa.

The local chiefs share with the Chinese the monopoly of the trade between Tibet and India as compensation. At present, as the treaty stands, it is necessary that we should engage in trade, though it does not yet yield any profit, but rather the contrary.

The following is an extract from the Regulation regarding trade, communications, and pasturage, to be appended to the *Sikkim-Tibet Convention of* 1893 :—

"(1) A trade-mart shall be established at Yatung, on the Tibetan side of the frontier, and shall be open to all British subjects for the purposes of trade from the first day of May, 1894."

The funds of the Mission and those used for trading purposes are distinct ; the drugs I generally dispense free. The trading is not a hardship. If Paul could make tents for Christ, surely we can do this for our Master. So those who are "called" to work for Tibet must be prepared for the present to sell goods to the Tibetans or attend to their ailments, as well as preach the Gospel to them. We are, first of all, *Missionaries* ; and this is well understood by the Tibetans and Chinese. The Tibetans would rather trade with us than with the Chinese, and willingly listen to the Gospel message. Naturally the Chinese do not welcome us ; for it is to their own interest to keep all Europeans out of Tibet, so as to secure the trade of Tibet for themselves as far as possible.

The Tibetans are a trustful, simple people ; and in the past the Chinese officials have influenced them against us — but lately their suspicions have been raised against the Chinese, because Narong, a large district of Tibet, has been annexed to the Chinese province of Szechuen, and it is now ruled by Chinese officials. The Grand La-

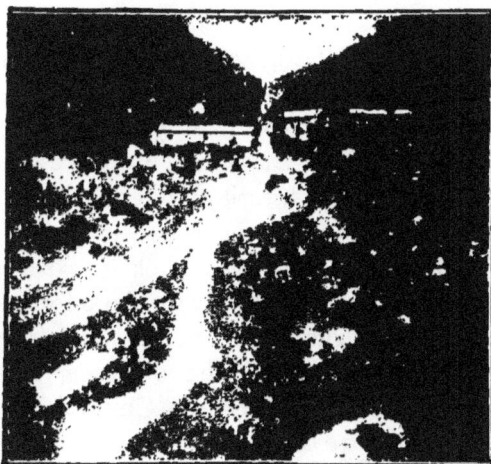

MISSION HOUSE.   CHIEF'S HOUSE.
JELAP PASS IN DISTANCE.

ma is now of age, and has taken the temporal government of Tibet into his own hands. The Chinese Emperor only acted as his guardian during his minority.

I have no doubt that Tibet will shortly be opened up without war, and that free intercourse will be established between Tibet and all other nations.

As regards my own personal expenses, I have now a small income of my own which meets them.

As the work and workers of the Tibetan Pioneer Mission

increase, so do the expenses ; but I feel sure that God, who
has so abundantly supplied all our need in the past through
His servants, will continue to do so in the future, and will
not suffer His daughters whom He has sent forth into that
cold, dark land of Tibet to suffer want.

Brethren, pray for us !

The following description of Yatung is from the pen of
Miss Ferguson, a member of the Mission :—

On arrival (April 3rd, 1896) it looked as if all the inhabitants were out to greet us, we being the first European
ladies to arrive here in English dress. Almost immediately
after the chief came to pay his respects and to present a
Khata (scarf of blessing) and a basket of eggs.

Yatung is built in a lovely valley at an elevation of
10,500 feet. Looking back towards the Jelap Pass, the
mountains are covered with dark forests of fir, above which
the snow peaks glitter, clearly defined against the deep blue
sky. Before us, in the distance, is the mountain range
lying to the north of the Chumbi Valley. The mountains
to the left are covered with grass and shrubs, and capped by
forests, on the crest of which a temple stands out con-
spicuously, surrounded by a number of quaint little houses
where the lamas live. To the right the mountains are
more precipitous and the forests are of birch, pine, and
other trees. The two mountain torrents, named Natui and
Langrang, which flow past Yatung on either side, join a few
paces below, and it is then called the Yatung River.

When in 1893 the Sikkim-Tibet Convention decided
that a trade mart should be established at Yatung, there
were no buildings here. Now they consist of the house
ostensibly built for the officer who might be appointed
by the Government of India to reside here, but occupied by

a Commissioner of the Chinese Imperial Customs, and
called the Custom House. This is a pretty two-storied
house surrounded by a verandah. Two native houses, one
occupied by the Tibetan Chief with his wife and a few
soldiers, the other by the Ropun (a Tibetan Chief of 250
soldiers who are scattered over the Chumbi Valley) his wife
and twelve soldiers, the Tibetan Clerk to the Chinese
Customs, and others. There are also one or two native
huts, and the sheds meant to serve as shops for British
traders, eighteen in number, which are joined together in
the shape of an oblong square. These have neither
doors nor windows, but are square sheds, with some of
the boards removed in the floor for a fire-place, and no
chimneys. The boards in front can be removed for
entrance. The gaping cracks let in the daylight. The
roofs are of wooden shingles held down by stones. These
are mostly occupied by Chinese, Tibetans, and Bhutanese.

Three of the sheds have been made by Miss Taylor,
with the help of her old Tibetan woodcutter, into a
shop (the only one in the so-called mart) and store-room,
a cosy little sitting-room, which I sometimes by mistake
call the kitchen, with a bedroom at each side, a kitchen,
larder, and small room occupied by Pontso (Miss Taylor's
faithful servant) and his wife. There are three small glass
windows in the sitting-room, and one in each of our tiny
bedrooms, which borrow their light from the sitting-room.
The only piece of furniture in each bedroom is a small bed-
stead, boxes serve for dressing table and washing stand.
The partitions between them and the sitting-room are of
half-inch planks, with gaps between, which allow of
ventilation.

Less than two hundred yards from Yatung the Chinese
have built a picturesque gate and stone wall, with battle-
ments and loop-holes, with an erection behind for the

defenders to stand on. The wall stretches across the valley and a short distance up the hills on either side. In a cluster of houses behind lives the Chinese military official in charge of the gate, and his twenty-five Chinese soldiers with their Tibetan wives and children. This barricade, beyond which no British subject is at present allowed to pass, along with the Custom House here, was built at the expense of the Chinese Government, whilst the sheds and other buildings in the mart were built at the expense of the Tibetan Government. And yet the Chinese would like us to believe that it is the Tibetans who keep us out, and go the length of saying in bland tones, how much they would like us to visit them further down the valley, were it not for "these ignorant Tibetans." I have often heard and read of the persistent effort on the part of the Chinese to keep the Europeans out of Tibet—now I see it. But we know that our God who is Almighty, and who has opened the door thus far, and given us a place in the hearts of the Tibetans, will ere long lead us forward.

In the Chumbi Valley there are twenty villages and over 3,000 inhabitants, many of whom find their way to Yatung for gospels and medicine.

Visitors and Present Surroundings.

The day after our arrival I put on the native dress, at which the Tibetans were delighted, and named me Anni Saba, or the new Anni. Miss Taylor is called Anni La. The literal translation of Anni is aunt, and is used as a term of respect for single women, as well as being the name given to Buddhist nuns.

We had a number of visitors, first the Tibetan chief of Yatung, who is very friendly. He was much interested in some photos which we had brought with us of our

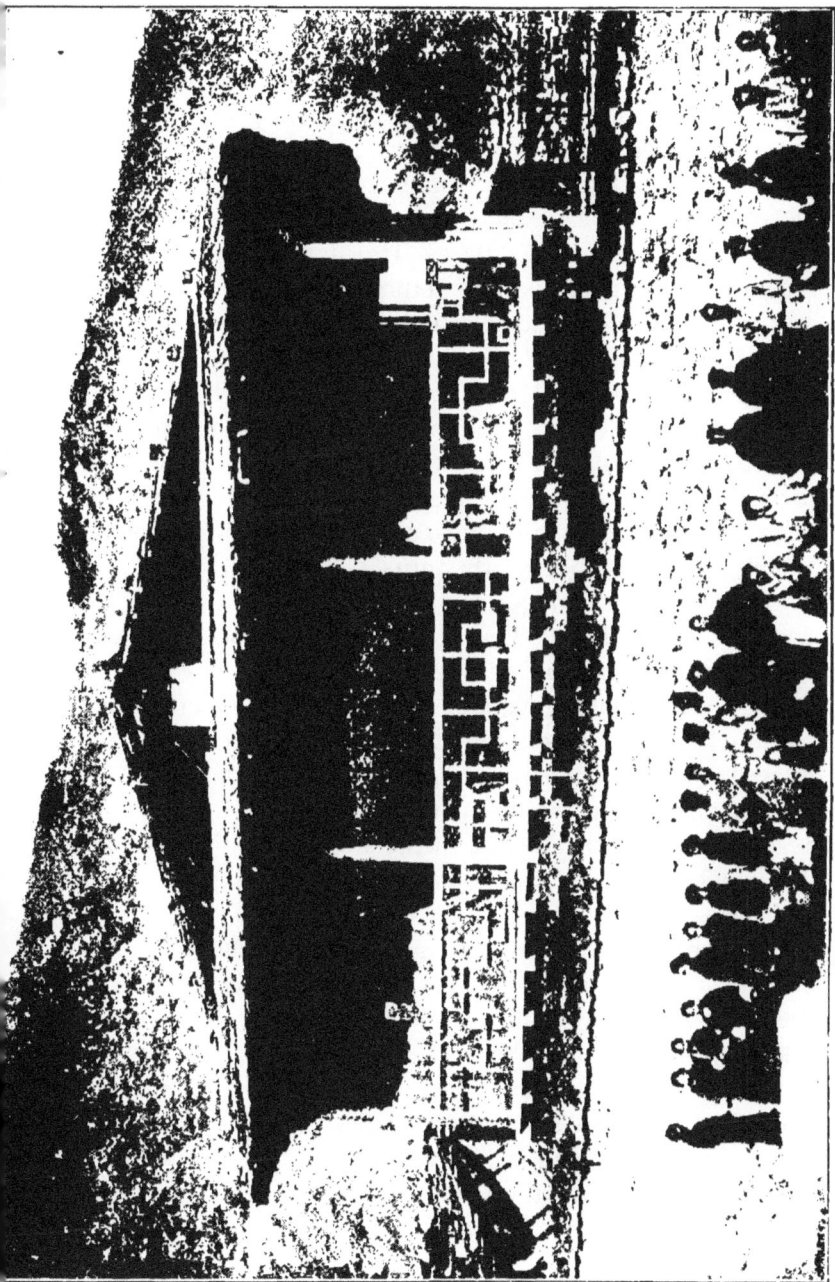

CHINESE CUSTOM HOUSE, YATUNG.

TIBETAN WOMEN.   CHINESE SOLDIERS.   TIBETAN CHIEFS.   TIBETAN SOLDIERS.

Queen and Royal family. Then, the Tibetan Clerk to the Chinese Customs, who is engaged to be my teacher, for I am to begin the study of the language on Monday. Afterwards, the Ropun, a Tibetan military official, and a number of soldiers. He is in charge of two hundred and fifty soldiers scattered over the valley. He and his men are from Shigatze and expect soon to return home, when an officer and men from Giangtse will take their places. The Ropun is an old man, with a short thin tapered beard, which is done up in a plait at his chin and tied at the end with a tiny cord and tassel. In one ear he wears a single turquoise stone, and in the other a pendant earring four inches long, composed of turquoise, pearl, and gold. He is usually dressed in silk, and carries a large silver prayer-wheel which he incessantly turns. Some of the soldiers wore coarse woollen gowns, and others the sheepskin so common in Tibet. They seem quite at home in our little sitting-room, and are evidently unconscious of the strong odour which emanates from their filthy persons and clothes. They are told the sweet story of the cross, and invited to come to Jesus; and it is cheering to hear from a Tibetan that the children were singing the hymn, "Yes, Jesus loves me," in Tibetan, in the streets of Shigatze. The soldiers had picked it up while here, and taught it to the little ones on their return.

The children of our little Mission day-school came as usual on Sunday, and Miss Taylor gave them a lesson from the picture of Christ blessing little children. They are so taken up with the news that He cares for little children.

A number of Tibetan women came to see us from down the valley. They carried their babies on their backs, tied on by shawls, Tibetan fashion. Some of them were natives of Lhassa, and had their hair dressed in two long plaits, and wore a coronet covered with red cloth, on which

turquoise, coral, and strings of small pearls are sewn.
Others have one long plait down the back, finished by a
heavy tassel which reaches to the ground; and a few
have from forty to over a hundred tiny plaits spread
across the back of the shoulders. Most of them had
their faces smeared with a kind of dark varnish, which is
looked upon as a mark of chastity. The native dress is a
long loose gown, crossed in front and caught up by a
girdle round the waist. Underneath is a cotton or silk
jacket, which shows at the neck and folds outside the
wide sleeve at the wrist to form a deep cuff: or is left
loose and falls beyond the tips of the fingers. The boots
are made of a variety of bright coloured cloths—blue,
scarlet, green, etc.—and are long and tied up under the
knee. The jewellery worn by the women consists of massive silver or gold earrings, set with turquoise or coral.
Large silver or gold amulets, studded with turquoise, are
suspended round the neck on a string of beads. Silver
chatelaines are hung from the shoulders, and bands of
silver encircle the waist, while numerous rings cover the
fingers. These dear women listened in wonder on hearing
of a present salvation and the enjoyments of heaven for
them, and said, "It might be for you, but how can it be
for us?"

An intelligent-looking lama from Cho-ni, near Miss
Taylor's old station on the Chinese border, came to see
us. He seemed much interested in the old, old story, and
delighted to get a gospel and some texts to take away
with him.

We paid a visit to the Tibetan chief and his wife, who
seemed very pleased to see us. He holds his appointment
directly under the government of Lhassa, and has to watch
over the Tibetan interests. He is the only official in the
district who can send letters direct to the Dalai lama and

government of Lhassa ; all others must send them through the · Chinese Amban stationed at Lhassa. Since he rented the sheds to Miss Taylor, he has been subjected to systematic persecution from the Chinese officials. This has led to the issue of an order from Lhassa, that all Tibetans living down the valley are to protect him in case of danger. Just lately, when things seemed threatening, he took refuge in our little mission parlour till the Rupon and some soldiers arrived.

YATUNG MEDICAL HALL.

On arriving at his house we climbed up a rude wooden ladder to the upper storey, and were shown into a large room and invited to sit on raised cushions —which we did in native fashion, with our feet tucked under us. On a low bench-like table before us incense was burning, and china cups, with silver saucers and lids, were set. These were soon filled with a concoction called tea, made from Chinese brick tea, mixed by churning, with salt, soda, and butter. I managed to drink it ; but not with a relish like Miss A. R. Taylor. Before we left, the postman arrived from Lhassa with a letter and some presents for the chief. The letter was wrapped in muslin and sealed, envelopes being dispensed with in Tibet. Letters are carried from Yatung to Lhassa in three and a half days. Travellers without much luggage can do the journey in a week ; heavily-laden caravans take more than twice that time. The storms of snow and hail which we have had since our arrival led the chief to remark that Jesus had given me good weather for my journey because I was coming to do God's work.

After being here a little while we paid a visit to the nearest temple, where the lamas received us in a friendly way ; one of them threw open the door of a building for us to see the prayer - wheels, forty-four in number, set on cylinders, and placed so that the worshippers can set them in motion, one after the other, as they walk along. Miss Taylor told them of the better way through Jesus, as

FRONT OF MISSION HOUSE, YATUNG.

they walked with us round the temple ; and presently we were joined by some Buddhist nuns from a little temple down the hill, one of whom accompanied us part of the way home ; and even while Miss Taylor was preaching Christ to her, from force of habit, once and again she repeated in a wailing tone the meaningless refrain, " *Om mani padme hum.*" Some of those nuns come to Yatung periodically to chant prayers and to beg. Miss Taylor sometimes asks them in and tells them of Jesus. They seem enchanted with the playing and singing of the sweet Tibetan hymns. Lamas

E

from a monastery built on rocks high up on the mountain often come between five and six in the morning and get their breakfast, etc., for chanting prayers and reading their Buddhist books in chorus for the supposed benefit of the inhabitants. These have received Gospels and Mrs. Grimke's texts in Tibetan to take away with them. Everything reminds us that we are in a heathen land—such as the numerous prayer-flags attached to long poles, as well as the strings of flags on the houses, stretched across the valleys and rivers, on the hilltops and chodtens. Chodtens are stone pyramids which contain the ashes of departed lamas, sacred books, and other relics.

When out for a walk we came to a shady nook by the side of a brook where some Tibetan women and children were bathing in a primitive bath, *viz.*, a scooped-out log. The icy water from the brook was heated by putting hot stones into the bath. These were made hot in a fire near by. The women lived in black tents, and one of them asked us to pay her a visit next day. So we went. The yâk with their black hairy coats and manes and long bushy tails were grazing on the brow of the hill, and the little calves were frolicking about, grunting like pigs. The barking of the fierce Tibetan dog brought out the woman to welcome us into her tent, which is woven of yâk's hair. The smoke from the wood fire makes the cloth greasy and so prevents the rain from coming through. The woman told us that the Gospel Miss Taylor had given her before had been begged from her by a lama. She has been to see us several times since, and never seems to tire of hearing about Jesus.

Sometimes our little Mission House is made quite lively by a number of Chinese visitors. The Ho-pun (Chinese Frontier Officer) and other Chinese officials come to Yatung on business, and with them a retinue of Chinese soldiers and servants, who visit us and hear the good news in their own language from Miss Taylor, and receive Gospels and calendars in Chinese to take back with them. It is cheering to hear them read and discuss in animated tones the Chinese tracts pasted outside our house.

When the Tibetan Frontier officer, the Chief of Phari Zong, and other Tibetan and Chinese officials come to see us, they are invariably dressed in bright coloured silks and satins ; the former are very dignified in appearance but very genial.

After I had been here about three weeks the old Rupon and his soldiers left Yatung. Many of the men came in to ask for Gospels to take back home with them to Shigatze. One of their number had died during their stay here, and his comrades, tying up his corpse in a worshipping position, took it down to Rinchengong and threw it in the river. He had heard the Gospel, and was much interested ; but whether he had found rest in Jesus or not we cannot tell.

The new Rupon, who has his wife with him, is a man of rank by birth, and may in time rise to have a seat in the Tibetan Government. As such he has his hair twisted in a knob on the top of his head, while other Tibetan officials wear their hair in a plait hanging down the back. He soon paid us a visit, accompanied by a number of soldiers, who quite crowded out our little room. They were charmed with the music from the organ. We heard afterwards that the Rupon and the chief had been reading and discussing the Gospel of St. John together.

A Prime Minister of Bhutan took refuge here lately on account of political trouble. His wife was exceedingly friendly and visited us repeatedly. When we called on them Miss Taylor took a copy of the Gospel of John and told them the simple story of Jesus. He listened most intelligently. The Bhutanese, both men and women, wear

their hair cut short. The men dress much like the Tibetans, but with a shorter robe. The women wear a shawl-
like dress wound round the body and fastened on the
shoulder with a brass or silver skewer. A cotton girdle
gathers it round the waist. When we visit the Tibetans
and Bhutanese we see them weaving woollen and cotton
cloth on rough hand looms.

Twice lately Tibetan soldiers have been assaulted by the
Chinese. In the first case the Chinese soldiers stationed
at the gate beat one of the Tibetan soldiers nearly to
death, because one of their number had had a quarrel with
him. And now one of the Chinese soldiers sent up by
the Ho-pun to Phari Zong to bring the rations, etc., killed
a Tibetan and seriously wounded two others, one of whom
is not expected to live. He is now a prisoner, but the
Tibetans say that all that is done by the Chinese in such
cases is, to send the offender to another place, pretending
they get him punished there. It is surprising to see how
long-suffering the Tibetans are.

One of the Tibetans, said to be a tool of the Chinese,
stopped the postman and took from him a letter addressed
to the chief here, which he opened and after acquainting
himself with the contents did it up again. Some who saw
him do it, afterwards reported it to the Tibetan frontier
officer, who sent him up here to be punished. He was
made to lie flat with his face on the ground and was beaten
by two soldiers in turn.

It was rather interesting in visiting one of the black tent
to find that an old woman and her son, in charge of the
yâk, had known Miss Taylor when she lived in the La-
Chen and La-Chong valleys, over six years ago. They
were drinking tea when we entered, and at once invited us
to be seated on a yâk's skin. The fire was burning on
the ground in the centre of the tent, with three stones

supporting the pot. Round the tent were oblong baskets in which all their goods and chattels are packed, and carried by the yâk when they move from pasture to pasture. A blown-out goat's skin hung from the roof, in which the milk is put and churned into butter by rolling it backwards and forwards on the ground. The usual wooden churn in which the tea is mixed was lying on one side. When the old woman had finished drinking her tea, she offered us some milk, and proceeded to wash out her wooden bowl and dry it on a filthy woollen apron. Miss Taylor suggested rinsing but not drying. This however did not satisfy her, but after finishing with the apron she drew a black towel from the bosom of her dress and completed the drying. We enjoyed the milk in spite of all. The boy had been reading a page out of one of their heathen books. Miss Taylor offered to exchange it for a Gospel if he would come for it, which he did next day.

When out walking we met the old woman, who told us that one of their yâk was missing, and she was going to Yatung to ask someone whom she knew to divine for her as to where it had gone. A few days ago the chief here got a spiritualist to enquire for him as to whether there would be war with the English or not, and as to his own future. The answer was, "Not for three years," and favourable as to himself. The Tibetans say that it is wrong to have intercourse with spirits; and yet, in times of uncertainty, they have recourse to so-called mediums, who seem to make a good thing out of it.

Wool and other caravans often encamp near here. These we visit and sit with the Tibetans around their camp fire. While they blow the fire with bellows made of a goat's skin, and make and drink their tea—to which butter of a green colour is added, that they seem to appreciate for its age and smell—Miss Taylor tells them of Jesus and sings to them Tibetan hymns, which they like to hear. The Gospels and texts given them are taken far into Tibet. Although the wool traders reside in this valley, the men they employ as mule drivers, etc., for the wool season, are from all parts of Tibet, a few coming even from Mongolia.

And now, in closing my letter, I ask you to praise God for thus thrusting me forth as another witness for Jesus into the land so long closed against the Gospel, and for shewing me a little of His working here. Numbers have heard the Gospel for the first time, while quite a few have been healed in the name of Jesus by the laying on of hands in answer to prayer. And I ask you to join dear Miss Taylor and me in definite prayer for the salvation of those who hear, and for me that I may soon be able to speak Tibetan.

With Christian love,

I am,

Yours waiting for the coming of our Lord,

BELLA FERGUSON.

Letters from Miss Foster.

(A Member of the Mission.)

"I WILL go before thee, and make the crooked places straight ; I will break in pieces the gates of brass, and cut in sunder the bars of iron " (Isa. xlv. 2). Such was the word the Lord gave me when He first laid missions to the heathen on my heart, long before Tibet crossed my thoughts. And now, within the first of those " gates of brass," and looking on in faith to those yet in front, we ask, " Who are ready to enter in when they shall be opened?" True, there is a cordon of devoted servants of the Lord right across the Indian frontier of Tibet, and round on the Chinese frontier ; but after all they are very few, compared with the mass of heathenism inside ; and the days are growing short, for the coming of the Lord draweth nigh. The language is acknowledged by all to be a very difficult one, and is known as yet to very few. And the heathenism ? I think people's impressions of the Tibetan religion are gathered very much from modern ideas of Theosophy and the Mahatmas. I have seen something of Buddhism in Ceylon, but any ideas I formed of it there have been rudely shattered here. As I sit here, with the door open, the glorious sunshine flooding the valley, the mountain slopes clothing themselves in every shade of green, while away above glitters the snow, I can echo again and again,

"Only man is vile."

Their only real belief seems to be a dread of evil spirits. And as I write, there comes to me the wearisome tinkling

of the lama's bell, and monotonous repetition of their senseless formula, "*Om mani padme hum*," of which no one knows
the real meaning.   All round the chief's house opposite,
and across the rude bridges that span our mountain torrents,
and on every point of vantage on these glorious mountains,
are strings of coloured rags—here and there white ones—
on which once these same characters were inscribed.   For
what, do you ask ?   These Tibetans believe that with every
flutter of the breeze these senseless rags, with their senseless,
washed-out inscription, lay up merit for those who hang them
there.   And looking into the Temple, we saw a row of
prayer-wheels, which are whirled round with the same object.
Truly this seems a stronghold of Satan.

And their prejudice and exclusiveness are as high as their
own mountain walls.   So it seems the more wonderful how
the Lord has in this place " cut in sunder these bars of iron."
The Tibetans come in and out freely, bringing all their
troubles, of whatsoever kind, bodily or otherwise, and take
with alacrity the medicine or advice given them.   Such is
their confidence, that the chief, who is very much at home
in our little sitting-room, tells us all the news that comes to
him from Lhassa and other parts of Tibet.   People come
here from great distances.   Last week the presence of some
special lama brought quite a number, and they all come in
to see the foreign Annis.   The women are distinguished
according to the district by their head-dress, and very funny
some of them are.   Few of those who come here ever cross
the pass into Sikkim, which is little to be wondered at, con-
sidering it is almost as high as Mont Blanc.   The little
organ and singing are always a delight to them, and none
ever come without being told of Jesus, the Mighty to save,
and none go without a copy of one of the Gospels, which
they take gladly.   Then the lamas in the monastery down
the valley welcome us, as do the people scattered about in

huts and tents.   And so here, just within the threshold of
Tibet, there is more work than we can do.

May I ask you, dear friends, to remember in prayer and
effort this dark corner, and also the one now left to hold the
fort, practically alone, and groping as yet on the confines
of the language.

Yours, in hope of His coming,

M. MARY FOSTER.

" AFTER THE EARTHQUAKE."

June 13*th*, 1897.

I do not think it likely that you will see telegrams in
the papers, headed " Fearful earthquake in Tibet—houses
and temples wrecked—lives lost," &c., and yet such is the
case.   Praise the Lord, we are all unhurt, so far ; and the
part of the house damaged is the least important, in a way.

The servants certainly cannot sleep in their usual places,
the wall is entirely gone.   My duplicated text, " The
beloved of the Lord shall dwell in safety," seems *very* real
now.   Praise His name, He keeps me in perfect peace.

Of course there are all sorts of reports and prognostica-
tions to-day.   However, there seem to be some facts.   One
is, that about ten houses in Rinchingong have fallen.   Another, that two men were killed by the falling of the barrier
at Galingka ; and the chief's wife says a great many were
killed at Chumbi, somewhere beyond Galingka.   Mr. Wang
says, the temple that we see is utterly down, only one bit
of the wall left.   Everything we hear only makes me praise
God it was no worse here.   Going round again, I see it is
only the wood-lining that saved all beyond the sitting-room
door.   The planks at the left side of the door are so bulged
by the fallen wall, that the door will not close ; and one
plank is held by one nail only.   But for that the wall would

have collapsed across the threshold and blocked me in yesterday. I had some more long nails put in to hold it till we see what is best to be done. After nine—I had breakfast at 7.30, for there was no staying quiet—I went up over the hill to look at the barrier. That on the right side, east, is simply a heap of rubbish. The big square house on the left side is unroofed; the soldier's house by the gate is a mass of ruins. Turning my glass on the monastery, I saw, as Mr. Wang said, it is an utter wreck; the "chutens" are all thrown down, and the parapets are swept clean off the Fort; only a low bit of wall remains. Those words kept ringing in my ears, "that those things which cannot be shaken may remain." There were the works that man "made" shaken to pieces, while the great mountains and trees, and all that God made, stood as quiet and firm as ever. And, as I sat and looked at that shattered wall, the thought came to me, " Does it not mean something, that in a few short minutes the hand of God has thrown down *both* the barrier walls--for they say Galingka is a more complete wreck than this one—and also the temple of heathenism that confronts the entrance to Tibet? How easily He has broken these 'gates of brass'—can He not as easily break the less material ones ? "

June 15th, 1897.

The remaining walls (*of the Mission house*) are in a dangerous condition. I am *very* tired : there has been no quiet from morning to night, people coming that had to be seen ; besides the tension, expecting a fresh shock every moment. We have had *eight* quite distinct ones, besides little tremors—none since five last evening.

The Tibetan Pioneer Mission.

Director - Miss ANNIE R. TAYLOR.

Address in Tibet.—Yatong, Tibet, *viâ* Darjeeling, India.

———

Referees:

Dr. T. J. BARNARDO, Stepney Causeway, London, E.

Rev. J. ELDER CUMMING, D.D., 14, Park Grove Terrace, Glasgow.

Rev. H. B. MACARTNEY, Melbourne, Victoria.

Miss MACPHERSON, Home of Industry, 29, Bethnal Green Rd., London, E.

JAMES E. MATHIESON, Esq., 58, Ladbroke Grove, Notting Hill.

R. C. MORGAN, Esq. (Editor of The Christian), 12, Paternoster Buildings, London, E.C.

Pastor H. RYLANDS-BROWN, The Manse, Darjeeling, India.

Rev. J. HUDSON TAYLOR, China Inland Mission, Newington Green, London.

ROBERT WILSON, Esq., Broughton Grange, Cockermouth.

———

Gifts may be addressed to Messrs. MORGAN & SCOTT, 12, Paternoster Buildings, London, E.C., who will acknowledge them in The Christian.

THE origin of the Mission was Miss Annie R. Taylor's journey in 1892–93 into Tibet proper, in the course of which she proved the possibility of gaining an entrance for the Gospel into that country so long believed to be closed to the emissaries of Christ.

The object of the Mission is to evangelize Tibet, and so remove one of the last barriers to the fulfilment of our Lord's words, "This Gospel of the Kingdom shall be preached in all the world for a witness unto all nations; and then shall the end come."

The field of operations is the country of Tibet itself, as far as entrance can be obtained into it, rather than the border tribes, amongst whom work is already commenced. Tibet, which lies north of India and west of China, is a large country, covering an area about ten times as great as England and Scotland together, and as yet we are the only Protestant Missionaries (so far as known) within its borders.

The field is a difficult one, although there is no marked hostility to the English on the part of the Tibetans. The Chinese Government Officials in Tibet are bitterly opposed to Europeans on account of the desire of the Chinese to keep the monopoly of Tibetan trade in their own hands. The climate is very cold, but dry and healthy, and any one proposing to offer for the work should possess a good circulation, and a constitution favourable to withstanding cold. The dwellings are primitive, being mostly huts and tents : and food is of the coarsest kind, except in the few scattered towns.

The language to be acquired is difficult when compared with Hindustani ; but the Moravians labouring in Little Tibet (which is under English protection) have compiled a dictionary and grammar of the Tibetan language, and translated into Tibetan all the New and part of the Old Testaments, thus removing at once one of the greatest difficulties generally experienced in a new country.

The principles upon which the Mission is worked are those of the China Inland Mission. But the main object of the Mission being to afford every Tibetan the opportunity of hearing the Gospel, it is purposed that the work of the Mission will be pioneering until such time as this object is acccomplished.

True-hearted and humble-minded men and women of God, full of the Holy Ghost and faith, experienced in Gospel work, and who have been used of God in winning souls, and holding the doctrines mentioned below, will be eligible as candidates, irrespective of what branch of the Church of Christ they belong to.

The Mission is supported entirely by the freewill offerings of the Lord's people. The needs of the work are laid before God in prayer, no personal solicitations or collections being authorized. No more is expended than is thus received, going into debt being considered inconsistent with the principle of entire dependence upon God. The director therefore cannot, and does not promise or guarantee any fixed amount of support to the workers. She seeks faithfully to distribute the funds available, and to meet the need of each worker; but they are expected to recognise that their dependence for the supply of all their need is on God, who called them, and for whom they have gone to labour, and not on the human organization.

It will be required that those who seek to join the Mission be sound in the faith on all the main points of Christian doctrine, which may be particularized as follows :—(1) The divine inspiration of the Scriptures ; (2) The Trinity of the Godhead; (3) The fall of man and his consequent need of regeneration ; (4) The atonement for man's sin ; (5) Justification by faith in Christ alone ; (6) The resurrection of the dead ; (7) The eternity of reward and punishment. They will also be asked to give their personal experience of the guidance of the Holy Spirit and the efficacy of prayer, as being points of importance in relation to the life of the missionary.

Candidates for the Mission are requested to communicate with Miss Taylor.

Brethren and sisters, " The harvest truly is great, but the labourers are few : pray ye therefore the Lord of the harvest, that He would send forth labourers into His harvest." And continue in prayer for Tibet ; for God says, "Ask of Me, and I shall give thee the heathen for thine inheritance, and the uttermost parts of the earth for thy possession."

HAVING seen much of Miss Taylor, and knowing that she has consecrated her life to the evangelization of Tibet, and admiring as we do her faith and zeal, we trust that she will soon secure two or three other devoted women as helpers.

The land for which she pleads must prove one of the most trying fields of Missionary labour ; but to those who have the physical and other qualifications for the work, and who are prepared to forget self, and seek only the advancement of the Redeemer's Kingdom, there is something specially inspiriting in the thought of being pioneers in so hard a field for the sake of Him who left heaven for the cross that He might save us. They will find that Miss Taylor will not ask them to endure any hardship from which she will herself shrink ; and her faith, devotedness, and experience, will be a stimulus to them. But we would especially urge that any who may think of responding to her appeal will carefully COUNT THE COST before-hand, try to put away all romantic ideas of Mission work, and to realize that work in Tibet means drudgery, privation, frequent disappointment, and patient, persevering toil.

G. H. ROUSE, D.D.

H. RYLANDS BROWN (Pastor).

Darjeeling, India.
May, 1895.

LONDON : MORGAN AND SCOTT, 12, PATERNOSTER BUILDINGS.

www.ingramcontent.com/pod-product-compliance
Lightning Source LLC
Chambersburg PA
CBHW020336090426
42735CB00009B/1562